THE KNOWLEDGE BASE OF CURRICULUM

An Empirical Analysis

Linda S. Behar
University of Florida

UNIVERSITY
PRESS OF
AMERICA

Lanham • New York • London

University Press of America,® Inc.
4720 Boston Way
Lanham, Maryland 20706

3 Henrietta Street
London WC2E 8LU England

Library of Congress Cataloging-in-Publication Data

Behar, Linda S.
The knowledge base of curriculum : an empirical analysis / by Linda
S. Behar.
p.   cm.
Includes bibliographical references and indexes.
1. Curriculum planning—Study and teaching (Higher)—United States.
2. Education—United States—Curricula.   3. Curriculum planning—
United States—Textbooks.   4. Curriculum evaluation—United States.
5. Curriculum change—United States.   6. Educational surveys—
United States.   I. Title.
LB2806.15.B44   1994   375'.001—dc20   93–26059 CIP

ISBN 0–8191–9266–X (cloth : alk. paper)
ISBN 0–8191–9267–8 (pbk : alk. paper)

∞™   The paper used in this publication meets the minimum requirements of
American National Standard for Information Sciences—Permanence
of Paper for Printed Library Materials, ANSI Z39.48–1984.

CONTENTS

TABLES

FIGURES

PREFACE

Knowledge bases are essential for disciplines. They assist practitioners and scholars in acquiring the fundamental tenets of a discipline and in making meaningful inquiry. In curriculum, knowledge bases help to clarify what educators actually do when they are engaged in planning, implementing, or evaluating curriculum phenomena.

The field of curriculum has endured criticism and misunderstanding because there has been a lack of agreement among curriculum scholars and practitioners regarding an agreed upon compendium of components or referents that describe curriculum activities and the methods or approaches that should be used to establish a knowledge base. The fluidity and vastness that characterizes the field have created difficulty in describing the field in consensually agreed upon terminology. Up to this point most discussions about knowledge base components have been largely qualitative and metaphorical in nature and have not provided empirical data to support the ideas presented.

Discussions and perceptions of curriculum might proceed to more sophisticated levels if an empirically defined compendium of behaviors or activities was provided that described what it is that educators do when they are engaged in curriculum related tasks in actual situations. This study represents an effort to establish a quantifiable knowledge base that was derived from curriculum textbooks published between 1970-1990.

Often students' first and or only acquaintance with a discipline is through textbooks. Given the central role that textbooks have been accorded, textbooks present a context for how learners will think about, interact with or interpret subject matter. Textbooks exert significant influence in guiding fundamental structures of disciplines. They can frame the impact of a course, and drive the curriculum either by serving as the content, or by exerting significant influence in shaping the curriculum.

What curriculum textbooks do the Professors of Curriculum think are most influential? What are the important domains of curriculum and the important behaviors and activities that curriculum workers engage in when doing actual curriculum work? Do teachers demonstrate agreement regarding the importance of curriculum practices as they pertain to specific domains? Is there a correlation between the curriculum practices that the Professors of Curriculum identify as important and the amount of coverage they receive in textbooks that the professors select? This research study was designed to investigate these questions.

Attempts to identify an empirical compendium of activities that describes what educators do when engaged in curriculum might evoke controversies. One might assume that the writer's views are embedded in a behavioral or prescriptive context. However, the findings herein are carefully grounded empirically and conceptually. Hopefully, the discussion and debate that might ensue as a result of this study will serve as a catalyst to advance the field beyond qualitative levels of inquiry. The field of curriculum seems to lack the status of a full fledged discipline. Perhaps the clearly delineated terminology and substantive data provided might partially ameliorate the absence of scientific evidence that has previously characterized the field.

It should be noted that in offering this quantifiable knowledge base, there is no intent to convey that qualitative components including the clinical, reflective, social contextual, humanistic, or relational aspects that occur alongside or within the curriculum are irrelevant. In fact, this would be quite contrary. Moreover, the field of curriculum needs to be defined in such a way, that colleges and universities have well-defined standards that describe what kinds of skills and behaviors students should acquire and will be able to use when doing various kinds of curriculum related activities as a result of professional study.

The knowledge base that will be discussed represents a macro framework depicting the types of activities that curriculum workers perform. It has broad application and is meant to outline the types of processes that curriculum workers engage in rather than the student or curriculum outcomes that may occur as a byproduct of the processes that they undertake. Viewing the results in this context will assist students, practitioners and scholars of curriculum to place the results of this study into their professional or work related schemata.

ACKNOWLEDGMENTS

I would like to thank a number of people who supported me during the time that I conducted the studies that formulated the central thesis of this book. I wish to acknowledge various groups of individuals whose participation made the book possible including: the members of the Professors of Curriculum, the teachers of Goethe School in Chicago, School, Melrose Park Elementary in Lake City, Florida and Crystal River Primary School in Crystal River, Florida.

I would also like to acknowledge friends and colleagues on the faculty and staff in the Department of Educational Leadership and the College of Education at the University of Florida.

I owe a special debt of thanks to my mentor, Allan Ornstein of Loyola University in Chicago and Ron Morgan also at Loyola, Andrea Brown, Jane Ganet-Sigel, Jack Pierce, and Richard Rotberg.

I want to thank family and friends, particularly Marilyn Behar and Emil J. Lauter and many others who I have not named specifically, but thank for their patience and belief.

Finally, I wish to acknowledge and thank the University Press of America for making this manuscript available to colleges, universities, curriculum directors, educators, and all curriculum workers who are devoted to making schools a place where all students can grow and experience academic success.

CHAPTER I

INTRODUCTION

This chapter is divided into six sections and describes: (1) an overview of the research study; (2) the purpose of the study; (3) the research questions; (4) the need for the study; (5) explications of the key components and terminology; and (6) a summary.

Background of the Study

This study was designed to establish a quantifiable knowledge base of domains and related curriculum practices. In addition, an attempt was made to determine if the Professors of Curriculum would select textbooks consistent with their viewpoints that they identified as being the most important, regarding the domains of curriculum. The domains of curriculum were divided into the following eleven areas of study: curriculum philosophy; curriculum theory; curriculum research; curriculum history; curriculum change; curriculum development; curriculum design; curriculum implementation; curriculum evaluation; curriculum policy; and curriculum as a field of study.

The study was conducted in three phases. In phase one, an open ended textbook survey was administered to a selected sample of the Professors of Curriculum (N = 88) to determine the most influential textbooks in the field of curriculum published between 1970- 1990. In phase two, a sample of urban elementary teachers in the Midwest

(MWTCHR), N = 48 and rural elementary teachers in the Southeast (SETCHR), N =37 were sent a survey and asked to rate the importance of the domains and related practices using a Likert scale. In phase three, using a close ended approach, a survey questionnaire was distributed to all of the Professors of Curriculum (N = 132) who were actively teaching and residing in the U.S. and Canada. The professors were given a list of the twelve textbooks identified as most influential. They were instructed to select one textbook and asked to: (1) rate the importance of curriculum practices; and (2) rate the extent to which curriculum practices within the domains of curriculum were covered within the selected textbook.

Purpose of the Study

This study was designed to establish a quantifiable knowledge base in curriculum and investigate the extent of agreement among the Professors of Curriculum in their determination of the most influential curriculum textbooks. The Professors of Curriculum conduct research, and are consultants to schools and education agencies. Elected to membership by invitation, they are considered to be major academicians in the field of curriculum studies. They often prepare future leaders by teaching courses that are germane to their training. It would seem desirable to analyze their empirical determinations of the curriculum domainsand related practices as well as the extent of their overall agreement in identifying the most influential curriculum textbooks. This determination might also be useful in clarifying the relative stability among the knowledge bases including: production; implementation; and appraisal systems within the field of curriculum. It is also desirable to survey other consumers of curriculum and textbooks, namely teachers, and assess their perceptions of the relative importance of various curriculum practices.

Textbooks are often students first acquaintance with a discipline. They are both purveyors and powerful determinants of how curriculum is used and understood. They influence how the learner will interact, conceptualize, or interpret the subject matter. Textbooks are instrumental in guiding students' mastery of the fundamental structures of disciplines. The selection of curriculum textbooks is an essential programmatic concern that can frame the impact of a course. Textbooks drive the curriculum either by serving as the content, or by exerting significant influence in shaping the curriculum.

Textbooks demonstrate the degree of consensus or fragmentation within a discipline. They provide direction for the field as a subject matter entity, and are instrumental in guiding students' mastery of the fundamental structures of disciplines. Curriculum textbooks perpetuate ideas about curriculum content that might influence curriculum systems in local school districts. Textbooks analyze and sometimes strongly advocate the ideas that practitioners espouse.

What curriculum textbooks do the Professors of Curriculum think are most influential? This research study addresses this question. A survey analysis of the most influential curriculum textbooks has not been undertaken since Shane (1981) rated the influence of one hundred selected works published between 1906-1981, Fraley (1981) identified twenty-nine curriculum classics published between 1894-1964, and Schubert (1984) discussed a chronology of 1,138 curriculum books written between 1900 and 1979.

Towards this end, this research study was designed to investigate the Professors' of Curriculum ratings of the importance of curriculum practices and extent to which curriculum practices within the domains of curriculum occurred in the most influential textbooks. This comparison a another dimension that can be used to document and useful and clarify the amount of consensus and fragmentation in the field of curriculum.

Research Questions

This research study addressed five research questions. Since there was no statistical procedure to determine the veracity or falsity of the first research question, it was examined using a descriptive analysis. Research questions two through five were analyzed using nonparametric statistical techniques.

1. To what extent do the Professors of Curriculum agree in their ratings of the most influential textbooks in curriculum?
2. To what extent do the Professors of Curriculum agree in their rankings of the most influential textbooks in curriculum in relationship to a) gender, b) doctorate specialization, c) year doctorate was earned, d) the geographical region of the institution where the doctorate was awarded, and e) the geographical region of their current institutional affiliation.
3. To what extent do the Midwestern teachers (MWTCHR) agree in their ratings of the importance of curriculum practices within the domains of curriculum?

4. To what extent do the Southeastern teachers (SETCHR) agree in their ratings of the importance of curriculum practices within the domains of curriculum?

5. To what extent do the Professors of Curriculum (PROFCURR) agree in their ratings of the importance and coverage of curriculum practices within the domains of curriculum?

Rationale for the Study

The essence of this study is to establish a knowledge base of curriculum practices within textbooks. Given the influential role of curriculum, attempting to specify a professional knowledge base for the field seems to be a timely consideration; it coincides with attempts in teacher education to define its purposes, practices and paradigms. A knowledge base of curriculum practices might provide educators with a focus for thinking about curriculum and instructional techniques.

Establishing a knowledge base will probably instigate controversy. The essence of a knowledge base requires that choices be made and judgments exercised. The sources of knowledge are also potential sources of error. In short, there can be no unassailable prescriptive set of beliefs resulting from a knowledge base. Evidence, conflicting conceptions and logical propositions must be weighted, selected, and synthesized into a coherent framework that renders the knowledge base usable for practice. By providing a systematic set of beliefs, knowledge bases also suggest ways of examining what is not yet discernible. The development of a knowledge base is therefore an evolutionary process that will be influenced by continuing reflection and as dispositions and empirical sources of knowledge emerge.

A study of this type is timely. To date, no other study has been conducted that examines the Professors' of Curriculum selection of the most influential textbooks, and simultaneously assesses the relationships among the Professors' of Curriculum ratings of curriculum practices within the domains of curriculum.

It is hoped that findings from this investigation will reveal basic data upon which to build improved programs for students seeking specialization in the field of curriculum. The ideas discussed and analyzed should be of some interest to the Professors of Curriculum. They might also be of some significance for researchers, and other professors in education responsible for studying, designing, and implementing programs in elementary, secondary, and higher education. Also, this study should have relevance for curriculum leaders and specialists. Finally, it should be noted that the components investigated in this study are broad, abstract ideas that taken together may set the framework or direction for other fields in education.

Conceptual Framework

In order to better understand the language used in this study, it seems necessary to describe the conceptual framework that supported this research project. This section discusses the conceptual framework and the key concepts underlying the research questions that were addressed in this study.

Definition of Key Components and Related Terms

Key components including: (1) **textbooks**; (2) **curriculum practice(item)**; (3) **knowledge bases**; (4) **domains of knowledge**; and (5) **domains of knowledge in curriculum (domains of curriculum)** are used throughout this research study. A definition for each term follows.

Textbook - A textbook is a book used for the study of a particular subject. It is a book designed to explain basic information of a field, including theory, research, and practice.

Curriculum practice (item) -- A curriculum practice is a statement that describes activities within the (eleven) domains of curriculum.

Knowledge bases -- Knowledge bases provide a compendium of technical skills and content knowledge that suggest what practitioners and scholars should know and be able to as a result of their training in a specific discipline. Knowledge bases provide a structure for making informed decisions and can be derived from works, that are composed of essential knowledge, established and current research findings, and sound practices such as textbooks. Knowledge bases can be defined in terms of classical topical categories, paradigms, or domains.

Domains of knowledge -- Domains of knowledge are ways of structuring the "knowledge base" of a field of study or a professional discipline. They are important content areas within a discipline that researchers and text authors examine in an attempt to further the field of knowledge.

Domains of knowledge in curriculum (hereafter referred to as domains of curriculum) -- These domains represent broad conceptualizations of curriculum that yield specific curriculum activities. The domains of curriculum for this study were eleven: (1) curriculum philosophy; (2) curriculum theory; (3) curriculum research; (4) curriculum history; (5) curriculum change; (6) curriculum development; (7) curriculum design; (8) curriculum implementation; (9) curriculum evaluation; (10) curriculum policy; and (11) curriculum as a field of study.

Domains of Curriculum

This section provides an operational definition for each of the curriculum domains that was identified using content analysis procedures of curriculum textbooks published between 1970-1990.

1. **Curriculum philosophy** is defined as a set of values, beliefs, and/or a particular orientation that determines an individual's broad view of a subject. It guides students, teachers, and schools in both teaching and learning. Inquiry into educational philosophy suggests a general view of students, society, as well as curriculum. Educational philosophy leads to a determination of educational theory, educational aims, and curriculum development and design.

Pertinent to the aims of curriculum philosophy are determining how conceptions of human nature, society, and values influence the views of education. This domain examines the quality of education, the meaning of equity in education and explores the standards, determined by personal, social, and national concerns that should be met by schools (Ornstein & Levine, 1989). Curriculum philosophy helps educators answer value-laden questions and make decisions among many choices.

The literature identifies five educational philosophies: (1) perennialism; (2) essentialism; (3) progressivism; (4) reconstructionism; and (5) existentialism (Doll, 1989; Ornstein & Hunkins, 1993).

2. **Curriculum theory** is defined as a set of related statements that give meaning to a school's curriculum by highlighting the relationships among important elements and by directing its development, use, and evaluation (Beauchamp, 1981).

Curriculum theory uses techniques of science and logic to identify fairly stringent rules that present a systematic view of phenomena. It is an activity that involves theorizing and reflecting which can also be interpreted as a process of clarifying meaning and the use of language (Schubert, 1986). McNeil (1990) divides the curricular theorists into two camps, the soft and the hard curriculum theorists.

The soft curricularists are concerned with understanding and revealing the political and moral aspects of curriculum making. Soft curricularists do not study change in behaviors or decision making in the classroom. They are concerned with ideas of temporality, transcendence, consciousness, and politics and their relationship to the process of education.

The hard curricularists assume that curriculum development occurs in response to an idea or vision of what ought to be taught. A series of logical choices or scientific justification determines the curriculum design. Empirical confirmation is the basis for justification.

3. **Curriculum research** is an activity used to: 1) advance conceptualizations and understanding of the field; 2) create new visions of what and how to teach; 3) influence curriculum policy; 4) question normative premises about curriculum; and 5) improve programs for learning (McNeil, 1990). Considered a mode of systematic inquiry for the purpose of solving a particular curriculum problem, curriculum research analyzes the steps to be taken in solving a given problem, tries one or more actions in line with that analysis, and then observes whether actions brought the results that were predicted or anticipated in the analysis (Doll, 1989).

4. **Curriculum history** is the process of describing, analyzing, and interpreting past curriculum thought and practice. Like history, it is a chronicle record of past events that may be represented by a narrative and/or an analysis of past events. By analyzing the past and the origins of curriculum, educators can better understand the present. A study of curriculum history can reveal insight and approaches to problems that relate to similar present day issues. An investigation of the forces that inhibited or promoted particular curriculum innovation, decisions, and action in the past can help educators analyze present conditions and plan future course of action (Schubert, 1986).

5. **Curriculum change** is an activity geared towards curriculum improvement. Curriculum developers are challenged with getting curriculum adopted at national, state, and local levels. Their plans must be accepted by textbook committees, curriculum commissions, boards of education, and others so that curriculum can be made available to teachers (Saylor, Alexander, & Lewis, 1981). Insuring that curriculum changes are properly implemented is another task. Some teachers might not be able to enact curriculum changes developed by others.

Implementing curriculum change should take into account the special knowledge and suggestions of those directly responsible for enacting the curriculum innovations (McNeil, 1990). For curriculum change to begin and endure, strategies for achieving cultural or institutional change are more significant than strategies for achieving technological change (Doll, 1989).

6. **Curriculum development** is the process of deciding what to teach and learn, along with the considerations needed to make such

decisions (Schubert, 1986). Integral to this effort is the identification of tasks, steps, roles, expectations, resources, time, and space, and the ordering of these elements into a system for carrying out the specified design to create a curriculum plan or document (Kimpston & Rogers, 1986). Curriculum development is an activity that determines how curriculum construction will proceed. The process addresses the questions of who will be involved in curriculum construction and what procedures will be used in this process.

7. **Curriculum design,** sometimes called curriculum organization is the arrangement of curriculum into substantiative entities. Generally, it consists of four components: (1) aims, goals, or objectives; (2) content; (3) learning experiences; and (4) evaluation approaches. Sources for curriculum design are the learner, science, society, knowledge, and in some cases the external/divine. Specific design dimensions include scope, articulation, balance, integration, sequence and continuity (Ornstein & Hunkins, 1993).

Curriculum design is a way of organizing curriculum ideas so they function in the real world of classrooms and schools. It might also be considered a carefully conceived plan that takes into account what its creators want done, what subject matter will be used, what instructional strategies will be used, and how the designer will determine the success or feasibility of the design. Diagnosis of need, organization and selection of subject matter and learning experiences are usually related tasks of curriculum design (Doll, 1989).

8. **Curriculum implementation** refers to the planning for and actual use of a curriculum in practice, and concerns the process of putting into effect the curriculum that was produced by construction and development (Kimpston & Rogers, 1986). Curriculum implementation by definition offers evaluative feedback to those in charge of the construction/developmental processes (Giroux, Penna & Pinar, 1981).

Curriculum implementation can be defined as a system of engineering that takes design specifications through various channels to the teacher and the classroom. It can be an interpretation of how well teachers carry out instruction in a school district. Curriculum implementation can refer to the development of learning experiences based on knowledge derived from the continuous interactions with learners (Schubert, 1986).

9. **Curriculum evaluation** is the process of answering questions of selection, adoption, support, and the worth of educational materials and activities (Scriven, 1967). Integral to curriculum evaluation is an emphasis on improving the curriculum (Stufflebeam, 1971).

Tyler (1949) delineates the task associated with curriculum evaluation as: (1) determining the effectiveness of curriculum content; (2)

measuring discrepancies between predetermined objectives and outcomes; (3) providing information about students' needs and capabilities; (4) guiding program development for individual students; (5) providing information about the success or effectiveness of curriculum content; (6) determining if objectives have been met and what changes took place as a result of the curriculum; (7) identifying strengths of curriculum content; (8) offering suggestions for modification; and (9) specifying curricular changes that need to be made with respect to content, instructional strategies, or methods that might lead to more effective curricular implementation.

Curriculum evaluation serves several purposes: 1) it provides a periodic assessment about the effectiveness of the curriculum, indicating changes that will facilitate improvement; 2) it influences teaching and learning by offering data essential to guiding individual students; and 3) it can validate hypotheses upon which curriculum selection and implementation operates (Madaus and Stufflebeam, 1989).

Curriculum evaluation is a continuous process that ascertains whether the planning, monitoring, and reporting of curricular activities regarding persons, procedures, and objects involved in actual situations have been achieved (Giroux, Penna & Pinar, 1981).

10. **Curriculum policy** is usually a written statement of what should be taught and serves as a guide to curriculum development. It establishes ground rules, limits, and criteria that circumscribe the curricula of educational institutions within a given jurisdiction. Curriculum policy must be determined by a democratic process whereby the wishes of all concerned parties are considered prior to legalization. (Saylor, Alexander, & Lewis 1981).

An authoritative allocation of competing values, curriculum policy addresses issues regarding graduation requirements, mandatory curriculum, and frameworks outlining the content for a field of knowledge (McNeil, 1990). Curriculum policy also addresses the question of what groups should influence the curriculum and to what extent. A mandate is a decision to promote one goal over another is an example of curriculum policy (McNeil, 1990).

11. **Curriculum as a field of study** is the combination of curriculum, the curriculum system, and research and theory building activities (English, 1983). Curriculum is the substantive or content dimension of curricular planning, implementing, and evaluation.

Zais (1976) defines curriculum as a field of study as the range of subject matters with which it is concerned (the substantive structure) and the procedures of inquiry and practice that it follows (the syntactical structure).

The curriculum field may be described as the subject matters that are treated in schools and the processes (for example, curriculum development, and curriculum change) with which specialists are concerned (Giroux, Penna & Pinar, 1981). According to Ornstein (1987), curriculum as a field of study, consists of its own foundations, domains of knowledge, research, theory, and principles.

The definitions of the domains of curriculum presented in this chapter formulated the basis for the items used in the survey questionnaire. All of the curriculum practices (items) listed in the survey questionnaire were taken from the context of the definitions that were discussed in this chapter.

Summary

This chapter presented a discussion of the background, purposes and research questions, as well as the need for this study. Definitions and discussion of the key components, including the textbooks, domains of curriculum, curriculum practices, and knowledge bases were discussed in relationship to the conceptual framework that served as the basis for this research project.

CHAPTER II

REVIEW OF RELATED LITERATURE

The overall purpose of this investigation was to establish an empirically defined knowledge base of curriculum practices within curriculum textbooks and identify the most influential textbooks in the field of curriculum. This chapter presents a review and discussion of literature regarding key terminology and concepts used in this study. Towards this end, an overview of four topics will be presented: (1) research studies of curriculum books that used survey methodology; (2) textbooks; (3) professional knowledge bases; and (4) domains of curriculum.

Survey Research Studies of Curriculum Books

A survey analysis of the most influential curriculum textbooks has not been undertaken since Shane's (1981), Fraley's (1981), and Schubert's (1984) studies. Shane (1981) reported the ratings of the influence of one hundred selected works published between 1906-1981. Using the Professors of Curriculum as respondents, he surveyed the 135 members and asked them to rate 100 designated publications that have appeared since 1906, and indicate whether the writing had major, considerable or negligible impact on curriculum theory and practice. Eighty-four professors responded to the survey. Weighted rankings were used to determine whether publications had major influence (2 points each) or considerable influence (1 point each). The publications that were ranked were not limited to the field of curriculum or just textbooks. Books in the field of educational psychology, education, counseling, and curriculum, as well as commissioned reports, and papers that focused on legal decisions were among the writings that were cited most frequently.

Fraley (1981) identified 29 curriculum classics that were published between 1894-1964. A classic was defined as a book that was a widely used reference, had a specific impact during its time, or functioned as a turning point document in curriculum theory development. The Professors of Curriculum were contacted to respond to a list that was circulated to members that attended the Professors of Curriculum meeting at the 1976 Annual Association for Supervision and Curriculum Development Conference. Fraley recommended that the list serve as a requirement for thorough study by all curriculum students, irrespective of their specialization before they continued too far into their graduate studies. She suggested that the list be regarded as either background for study of current writings or collateral writings emphasized in specialized course work, rather than as a total program requirement.

Schubert (1984) identified a chronology of 1,138 curriculum books that appeared in America from 1900 to 1979. Monographs and yearbooks, journal articles in books of curriculum readings, and educational journals that devoted entire issues to curriculum matters were also included. The criterion for including a book in his listing was based on the determination that the book dealt with some aspect of curriculum. Books that had curriculum in their title were included. Books that addressed specialized content areas such as special education or science were excluded. However, certain books that didn't have curriculum in the title but focused on issues such as deciding what to teach or learn, or determining how people should determine what to teach others, were also included among the survey citations.

Textbooks

In this section a discussion of textbooks related to the conceptual framework of this research study is presented. This section begins with a review of studies that have identified influential curriculum books using survey methodology. The discussion of textbooks proceeds with an overview of research and related literature of areas that represent a continuing concern to educators and researchers. This discussion focuses on three topics: (1) advantages and disadvantages of textbooks; (2) how textbooks influence learning; and (3) selection and adoption of textbooks. It should be noted that this review is not meant to be exhaustive.

Advantages and Disadvantages of Textbooks

Textbooks are a powerful force in American education and reflect the dominant social, political, and moral values that pervade at the time of their selection and publication. How textbooks get selected, who selects them, and for what purposes they are created is really not entirely democratic. Choosing a textbook requires a multitude of approvals that must satisfy many segments of people simultaneously (Cole & Sticht, 1981).

Textbooks provide a level of content expertise in an organized and logical format that few teachers possess. They facilitate the teacher's instruction by mapping out the journey that the teacher and student will share. A companion teacher's guide that provides discussion questions, activities, worksheets, test items, and answer keys usually supplements the textbook. Textbooks allow teachers additional time to plan for instruction since they have already defined the aims and sequence of curriculum (Eisner, 1985).

Advantageous to both educators and students, textbooks provide: (1) a uniform mode for course study; (2) a synthesis of material in a systematic and organized format; (3) visual presentations to facilitate understanding of the structures of a discipline; (4) an outline that teachers can use for planning courses, units and lessons; and (5) ready made curriculum that allows teachers more time for preparing course materials (Ornstein, 1990). Textbooks should be considered a central force in the process of acquiring knowledge whereby they form both the hub and link to other sources, hands-on activities, supplementary materials, and experiences that will render the curriculum an active and relevant experience for all students. Curriculum must become a practical, kinesthetic, auditory, and visual experience for students if it is to be relevant and applicable.

Textbooks are a major factor in shaping instructional programs. Commercially published multigrade packages comprise a virtual national curriculum in public elementary and junior high schools (Woodward & Elliot, 1990). Woodward and Elliot (1990) claim that many present day teachers would have difficulty maintaining instructional programs in basic subjects without multigrade textbooks. Additionally, textbook programs also serve as training tools for novice teachers who lack instructional expertise in specific subject areas.

Textbooks are a dominant influence in the classroom; they seem to determine content and teaching practices (Tulley and Farr 1990).

Students need to learn to work with a wide range of instructional materials and teachers must utilize a variety of resource materials to meet students' comprehensive needs. Textbooks serve as a valuable instructional tool too, but they should not constitute the principal source of curriculum guides and lesson plans, nor should they be the sole medium for instruction. Instead, they should serve as the catalyst for instruction (Tanner, 1988). In spite of the author's attempts to maintain objectivity, students might still be the recipients of the author's personal viewpoints and biases. Textbooks are written to generate profit and simultaneously meet educational needs of masses. Because of the need to appeal to large markets, textbooks may fail to represent certain populations, may omit controversial, complex, or value-laden topics, and may demonstrate conceptual simplicity. They are often criticized for a lack of significant inquiry, depth and sophistication necessary to fully explain basic concepts, principles, and ideas (Ornstein, 1990).

Controversial issues are frequently defused or omitted by textbook publishers seeking a wide market. The nation's capacity for growth is a function of the amount of intellectual tolerance it affords those whose beliefs are inconsistent with the consensual viewpoints. Assessing the motives of textbook publishers should be open to analysis to decide whether they are profit-oriented, conformity-seeking, or designed to provide the broadest range of intellectual perspectives for our students (Eisner, 1987).

Publishers have been forced to write and adapt textbooks according to readability formulas (Bernstein, 1985). Readability formulas are estimates of readability. They tend to measure sentence and word length and in some instances uncommon words (Schmidt, 1981). Schmidt claims that readability formulas should not be the sole basis for selecting or rejecting textbooks. Readability formulas neglect characteristics of readers that affect comprehension including their background knowledge, motivation, interest, and perseverance. Additionally, readability formulas fail to consider many characteristics of the text that are important in comprehension and learning (Anderson & Armbuster, 1988). While readability levels are important factors in determining the appropriateness of materials for the grade levels at which they will be introduced, they are not the only means to assess the appropriateness of materials.

Criticism has been leveled against publishers for blindly responding to demands for adherence to readability formulas (Bernstein, 1985;

Keith, 1985). Such formulas have been cited for a decline in the use of prose and stylistic qualities that seem critical to students' motivation to read, and lend textbooks to comprehension. Readability formulas have also been cited as a contributing factor to students' decline in higher order thinking abilities (Bernstein, 1985).

Thompson (1987) offers a process-product model that relies on system analysis of the textbook universe. She used the concept of megasystems to explain the textbook writing process. Her model indicates that there is an interaction among varied autonomous, but interdependent "peer systems" including the family, government, knowledge production, school, and knowledge distribution systems (Thompson, 1987). Peripheral but influential "satellite systems" also affect textbooks. Among the systems are parent and teachers' organizations, religious bodies, and self constituted textbook critics.

In this connection, college texts are sometimes criticized for their lack of depth, omitting contemporary macro-level societal phenomena in favor of student interest and readability, not offering summaries and syntheses of research, not acknowledging controversy within the field, and the ambiguity in the knowledge base (Perrucci, 1982).

Contributing to the failure of excellence in textbooks are economic priorities of publishers, the existence of mass lecture sessions as the main teaching tool in large universities that are related to the use of comprehensive texts, and constraints on authors that are inherent in the publication of manuscripts. Perrucci (1982) reports that constraints on the authors include the pressure of producing a final manuscript on time, the author's ability to integrate critical reactions of reviewers to the first draft, and dealing with one's own ego strength to endure appropriate criticism. Another factor contributing to textbook inadequacy is the need to create textbooks that cater to the growing number of students today who are unable to read at college level. Writing easier textbooks that compensate for alleged deficiencies of students means using short sentences, short words, many headings, numerous illustrations, and undemanding content (Perucci, 1982).

Textbooks are influential vehicles for disseminating knowledge. Should they be held in such high esteem? Are instructors overly dependent upon the gospel of textbooks? Are current methods of assessment sufficient to ensure the adequacy and accuracy of content portrayed in textbooks?

Armbuster and Anderson (1988) found that many elementary and intermediate science and social studies textbooks lacked global and section signals, such as headings, subheadings, format clues, signal words, and phrases that are important aspects of coherent organization.

They also observed that the textbooks failed to convey the inherent content relationships. Armbuster and Anderson (1988) suggested that the lack of cohesiveness resulted from the publishers' dependence on readability formulas. They observed that the impact of making a text easier to read resulted in: (1) rendering the text more difficult to understand; (2) abrupt and confusing topic transitions; and (3) a lack of connectedness between graphic aids and textbook prose.

Textbooks have been identified as a major contributor to the ignorance of school-age American youth regarding the important concepts and knowledge in economics, history, geography, and science (Cheney, 1988, Ravitch and Finn, 1987). Tyson and Woodward (1988) point out that the poor quality of social studies and history textbooks have been cited as a factor in failing to interest students in subjects that many critics see as interesting and exciting. Sewall (1988) observed that the market conditions and a lack of subject matter expertise among authors, consultants, and textbook selection committees have contributed to stilted prose and students' inability to connect isolated facts and larger patterns of history. The failure of textbooks to keep up with new knowledge has contributed to students' misinformation. Inaccuracies have been caused by compression, misconception, and the avoidance of controversial issues.

A study published in 1983 examined ten introductory psychology textbooks and five social psychology textbooks (Bertilson, 1983). The findings of this study suggest the following: (1) growth of knowledge base confounds the problems of accuracy and consensus; (2) the problem of validation of textbook accuracy may result from the absence of means to ensure accuracy; and (3) defining a concept without critical evaluation leaves a false impression that the concept is accurate or valid (Bertilson, 1983).

Inaccuracy sometimes occurs because of pressures from publishers for the completion of the final manuscript and the absence of controls that would ensure accuracy of textbook content (Bertilson, 1983). Attempts at broad coverage can create erroneous impressions when certain topics are treated superficially. Textbooks should strive for depth and breadth rather than providing superficial coverage of many topics.

How Textbooks Influence Learning

Textbooks define much of the content, sequence, and aims of curriculum. They provide an overview of a particular body of knowledge for students with little to no background in a specific discipline. Because students lack previous experience in a subject, they are especially reliant on the text structure to show them how to construct schemata or visual image for thinking about the subject matter and incorporating it into their experiences (Hubbuch, 1989). Eisner (1985) maintains that textbooks are responsible for influencing ways in which topics will be received by students, and determining the extent to which students will engage in content-related studies. The textbook has a poignant effect on students' motivational level, willingness to study subject matter, and likelihood of learning structures of various disciplines (Eisner, 1985). Textbooks are instrumental in influencing what should be taught in schools. The influence of textbooks can not be underestimated; children's first experiences with books may shape their attitudes toward reading for the rest of their lives (Bernstein, 1985; Keith, 1985).

By providing the nucleus around which much of what is taught, textbooks determine and direct the nature and sequence of instruction. They have significant impact upon the learning experiences of students. They promulgate stress on the written word as a main mode of education. Many times, the textbook is the only perspective that students receive in a course (Ornstein, 1990).

Important purveyors of curriculum, textbooks influence curriculum and determine course content. Sometimes they constitute the course content. Content has become equated with material to be covered in the textbooks. Much of what students receive through their studies at the elementary, secondary, and postsecondary level is contingent upon the textbooks selected for their studies. Textbooks discuss the basic syntax, tenets, foundation, and important areas of content within a given discipline. They assist students in acquiring the basic structures of knowledge, that otherwise remain unavailable through ordinary experiences and influence the way certain topics will be regarded (Eisner, 1987).

Scholars guide the construction of textbooks in subject areas because it is assumed they have the expertise to do so. (Schubert, 1986). They play an important role in conveying the basic structures of disciplines. Subject matter takes for granted that curriculum is a matter of pre specification by relegating content solely to the disciplines of knowledge. Curricular content, namely the subject matter, is derived from the disciplines of knowledge. Textbooks remain the dominant mode of content delivery, accounting for up to 80 percent of subject matter to which students are exposed in a typical course of study (Schubert, 1986; English, 1980).

Researchers studying learning strategies have observed that textbooks often contribute to students' comprehension and learning difficulties.

Hubbuch (1989) suggests that inconsiderate textbooks reinforce students' passivity in learning, retard their ability to think critically and analyze important social, political, and ethical societal issues. Making teachers aware of the qualities of inconsiderate and poorly written texts allows them to prepare students for difficulties they'll encounter in upcoming text passages and helps them instruct students in ways that facilitate coping with difficult texts (Duin & Prenn, 1985).

Duin & Prenn (1985) suggests that teachers use the following four factors when evaluating texts: (1) structure - the arrangement of ideas and the relationships connecting them; (2) coherence - the smoothness of logic which ideas are woven together, or the flow of meaning; (3) unity - the degree to which the text addresses a single topic; and (4) audience appropriateness - the extent to which the text matches the reader's knowledge and interest.

By studying the students' use of textbooks, or the impact of influential textbooks, we are in fact studying only one part of a system that has its own evolving history (Cole & Sticht, 1981). Sticht (1981) asserts that each new generation of teachers shapes the learning of students vis a vis teachers' experience as students. Each subsequent cohort of textbook authors writes with an implicit understanding of teacher and student audiences, with expectations of how teachers will utilize their writings, and how students will synthesize the content for their own cognitive and/or affective growth.

In order to fully appreciate the role of the textbook as an instructional tool, one must be aware of the complex system in which it functions. This necessitates inquiry into the students' use of texts that may also provide information about how to improve students' use of texts and make them more usable. To some degree, the students' use of text, will be conditioned by the teacher's use of the text. The cultural environment also effects the text-teacher-student system in ways that are not fully comprehended.

Studying the ways in which teachers use textbooks can provide a different conception of the ways in which textbooks influence learning. According to the National Commission of Excellence in Education (1983), textbooks have been regarded as a villain and cure in what many perceive as a crisis in education. *A Nation at Risk* called attention to the need for more rigorous examination of textbook content and research on how textbooks are used in classrooms. Other researchers have suggested that teaching and learning are directly linked to the nature and content of textbooks (Tyson-Bernstein, 1988; Tyson & Woodward, 1989; Woodward & Elliot, 1990).

Using four fourth grade teachers in 2 urban schools in a single district, Sosniak and Stodolsky (1993) studied their use and thinking about instructional materials. Their findings revealed that the teachers displayed more autonomy in the use of textbooks than the literature regarding the state of elementary education has indicated. Teachers did considerable selecting from, reorganizing of, and adding to textbooks without concern or self-consciousness about the way they used textbooks. Textbooks served as props and curricular embodiments in the service of managing instruction rather than as a driving force for the curriculum.

On the basis of their findings, Sosniak and Stodolosky (1993) concluded that textbooks do not control the elementary curriculum to the extent ordinarily assumed and nor does textbook content necessarily directly influence learning. They recommended that further study and training that engages teachers in a more explicit examination of how they use textbooks as well as the role that textbooks play in planning and carrying out curricular goals and instructional agendas would contribute to the development of more accomplished teachers.

Selection and Adoption of Textbooks

The selection and adoption of textbooks are crucial concerns for educators because textbooks are a primary instructional medium and they also provide students with an education lifeline (Bernstein, 1988; Keith, 1985). The particular practices that influence textbook adoption are closely related to national conventions which influence the direction of curricula and teaching the different ends that nations seek as they direct and order the work of schools (Husen & Postlethwaite, 1985). Keith (1985) points out that there are no federal regulations mandating what a state is to teach, or not teach, or federal guidelines legislating the way public educational materials are to be selected. It is within the jurisdiction of each state to define how instructional materials will be selected.

Noncurriculum issues play an important role in textbook approval policies. These issues may be particular to the time when the textbook has emerged. Approval of textbooks may be contingent upon the availability of state funds and the physical durability of the textbook, or subject to state monitoring to assess the extent to which "appropriate" national concerns are being communicated. Approval may produce many "approved" textbooks or only one or two for each subject area (Husen & Postlethwaite, 1985).

Effective instruction depends greatly upon matching materials with the teaching styles of instructors and the cognitive styles of learning. Textbooks should be selected by teachers who will use them because they know their student groups best (Bernstein, 1988; Warming, 1982). However, it is the teacher's level of effective usage of the textbooks that may ultimately influence pupil achievement.

There are basically two types of textbook adoption procedures in the United States, nonadoption or open territory states, and adoption states (Bernstein, 1988; Keith, 1985; Tulley and Farr, 1985). In the twenty-eight nonadoption states, textbooks are selected by local school districts (Bernstein, 1988, Keith, 1985, Tulley & Farr, 1985). It is assumed that the nonadoption approach states minimizes controversy and allows maximum flexibility to school districts in identifying their choice of textbooks (Keith, 1985).

A state adoption system is operative in 22 states (Bernstein, 1988; Keith, 1985; Tulley and Farr, 1985). With the exception of California and Oregon, adoption states tend to be located in the South and Southwest regions of the country (Keith, 1985). There is diversity in the selection process and in the number of books that may be purchased with state funds in these states. The decisions relating to textbooks to be included in adoption are usually the responsibility of lay committees. Length of adoption time varies from two to six years and the adoption list for a basic series may vary from two to several choices.

Tulley and Farr (1985) cite three advantages continually thought to be associated with state level processes: (1) uniformity of curriculum; (2) reduction of textbook costs because of contractual agreements between states and publishing companies; and (3) periodic reviews and updating of textbooks.

The strength of the adoption system lies in its diversity (Cole & Sticht, 1981). The system has an obligation to remove offensive material, but also is mandated to provide equal treatment of the sexes and full representation of minorities. The textbook adoption system should be sensitive to omitting bias from publication. Among the system's greatest weaknesses is that is not easily open to change nor does it demonstrate a willingness to innovate and experiment.

The impact of a few state adoptions regarding curriculum and textbook content upon the nation is substantial. Several researchers have noted that Texas, Florida, and California account for a sizable portion of the national textbook market (Bernstein, 1988; Keith, 1985; Ornstein & Hunkins, 1993). Textbook publishers are responsive to mandatory state curricula objectives as well as format and binding regulations. By incorporating the textbooks requirements of these three states and other large adoption states, constraints are imposed on the distribution of textbooks nationwide. The textbook industry is a highly competitive industry, but it is subject to the vicissitudes of the market, student demographics, and government regulations. Textbook adoption and selection must balance the complexities between the written word, pedagogy, and subject matter and between desirable goals and regulations imposed by states.

Exploring the politics of curriculum decisions and how they are manifested through selection and adoption of textbooks in the state of Texas was the subject of Marshall's (1986) study. Using primary document, survey, and oral history data, he determined how state-level textbook decisions were made during the period 1969-1981.

Marshall explored the actions of participants in three decision groups: the state textbook committee; the state board of education; the commissioner of education and his staff; and their interactions with textbook publishers and petitioners (protesters). The results of Marshall's (1986) study indicated that while all three groups used the Texas guidelines as evaluation criteria, each group interpreted them differently. Publishers were most influential with the state textbook committee and least influential with the board of education. Petitioners were most influential with board members and less influential with the textbook committee and the commissioner of education and his staff.

American publishers are not autonomous enterprises (Bernstein, 1988, Keith, 1985; Cole & Sticht, 1981). Existing in a symbiotic relationship with teachers, schools, textbook selection committees, educational researchers and curriculum specialists, publishers are subject to complex systems of constraints and responsibilities (Bernstein, 1988, Keith, 1985; Cole & Sticht, 1981).

Textbooks serve as indirect means for establishing national educational standards for children, teachers, and school districts (Keith, 1985; Cole & Sticht, 1981). While schools may be locally and state controlled, textbooks are written for a national audience. Although publishers do not write curriculum, nor do they attempt large scale curriculum reform, they respond to changing requirements by providing new or revised textbooks that reflect changing priorities among school districts. Along with teachers, educational researchers and curriculum specialists, textbook selection committees constitute one of the most powerful forces for the influencing educational achievement

The 1970s and 1980s were witness to vast changes in the selection procedures for textbooks. Enhanced by militancy and demands from teachers to participate in key instructional decisions, the selection process has progressed from using a small group of informed teachers and administrators through an arduous process of analysis toward greater involvement of many more individuals and a greater number of teachers (Cole & Sticht, 1981).

Changes in textbooks and instructional materials are clearly related to funds available for school expenditures. Textbook innovations can be financed only to the extent that they can be formatted within the context of available funds (Cole & Sticht, 1981). Komoski (1980) reported numerous problems with the textbook selection process. Based on a six year assessment of instructional materials used in the United States, the Educational Products Information Exchange (EPIE) concluded that the selection of textbooks and other materials currently practiced in most schools is producing an instructional mismatch of materials to learners' capabilities. Commercially marketed materials tend to structure and often define the classroom curriculum, a situation which does not guarantee instructional effectiveness.

EPIE testified to Congress, that 99 percent of the materials being bought by school had never been field tested or revised on the basis of learner feedback. A current EPIE REPORT, devoted to the aim of improving text materials through learner verification and revision, reported that excellent efforts were being made by a few publishers to better fit learner needs through testing and revising their products. However, most publishers surveyed were not doing much about improving materials based on learner feedback. Schools continue to spend untold sums on untested, unimproved materials that are not matched to learner's needs.

Textbooks need to be evaluated by scholars and professional staff to ascertain whether they meet qualitative criteria as determined by the best available evidence in the professional literature (Tanner, 1988). Tulley and Farr (1990) recommend that: (1) textbook adoption be conducted at the local level rather than at the state level; (2) specific criteria be developed to guide textbook review; and (3) individuals responsible for the selection of textbooks receive thorough training in review and evaluation procedures. Cody (1990) also concurs with the notion that school boards take a more active role in the textbook selection process.

Bernstein (1988) recommends that: (1) adoption state policy makers abandon the use of readability formulas as adoption criteria; (2) appoint people to serve on adoption committees solely on the basis of their knowledge and talents; (3) provide substantive training for adoption committee members; (4) hire teachers to serve on adoption committees; and (5) establish subject specific policy framework for curriculum review. In contrast to these views, Keith (1985) questions the merit of a textbook approach and suggests that the hegemony of the textbook as the dominant mode of content dissemination be reexamined. Tanner (1988) supports the notion that greater attention needs to be given in programs of preservice and inservice teacher education to the selection and uses of textbook. One of the principal criteria in evaluating a textbook must be the extent to which it interfaces with other studies in the total school curriculum. Textbooks should be adopted and used as though subject matter were interdependent, working harmoniously through an interdisciplinary network rather than as isolated entities and independent knowledge compartments.

Professional Knowledge Bases

The field of education, particularly teacher education, is undergoing tremendous transitions, in an effort to identify a knowledge base. Knowledge bases that are pertinent to teacher education may be conceptualized in terms of classical topical categories, research domains, and paradigms of teacher education (Gideonse, 1989).

In teacher education, knowledge bases include different ways of knowing that are important for teachers and necessary for practice (Gudmundsdottir, 1991). To assist teacher education in defining a knowledge base, five attributes are defined: (1) a set of beliefs; (2) an organizing theme; (3) program outcomes and evaluation processes; (4) a bibliography of essential references; and (5) program models (Galluzo and Pankratz, 1990). A set of beliefs serves to guide program development. An organizing theme is the unifying concept that represents the essence of the set of beliefs. Program outcomes are descriptions of the knowledge skills and attributes that teacher education graduates should possess. The evaluation component functions as the process for student assessment and program evaluation. The bibliography should be comprised of collectively agreed upon source documents that contain essential knowledge to be learned by graduates of the program. This body of literature should summarize key concepts and principles from research, theory, and practice. Program models serve as graphical representation and/or verbal descriptions that show how conceptual elements form an integrated program (Galluzo and Pankratz, 1990).

Knowledge bases provide a theoretical framework that is comprised of essential knowledge, research findings, and sound practices that provide a structure for making informed decisions. A knowledge base must consist of a collectively held and systematically reinforced set of beliefs that guide program development and instruction. Central to the formulation of a knowledge base are the development of beliefs about the purpose of schools and the roles of teachers, educational philosophies, theories and research, social perspectives, educational practices, research on teaching, and contemporary societal concerns. (Galluzo and Pankratz, 1990).

A knowledge base is developed from source documents. The domains of curriculum selected for this investigation represent a potential knowledge base of curriculum practices. Classical topical categories were systematically selected from references that serve to undergird their inclusion. The domains of curriculum were selected from bibliographic sources that promulgate essential knowledge in the areas of theory, practice, and research. The bibliographic sources from which the domains of curriculum were derived represent a potential bibliography.

Curriculum is the umbrella that guides teacher education. It influences design and delivery of effective professional education programs. Programs must be grounded by a knowledge base that forms an authoritative structure which offers a platform of concepts, facts, and principles that guide development and inquiry of a given discipline. Knowledge arises from processes of design, decision, intuition, and empirical inquiry (Gideonse, 1989). Knowledge bases serve to define purpose. Purpose is a key organizing principle and a primary consideration before any type of instruction can take place.

Domains of Curriculum

There appears to be scarcity of research studies that have investigated domains of curriculum. However, a few researchers alluded to the relationship, and the importance of it. Beauchamp (1981) was one of the first theorists to analyze curriculum in terms of domains, which he called "curriculum knowledge", into planning, implementing, and evaluating. Foshay and Beilin (1969) used the term "curriculum knowledge" and divided curriculum into theory, design, and change.

Rosales-Dordelly and Short's (1985) descriptive study sought to investigate the degree of similarity among 95 General Curriculum Professors in the U.S. and Canada in indicating three things about 36 selected curriculum references: how the professors understood and classified knowledge into various domains of curriculum; in what contexts they utilized curriculum knowledge in their academic work; and what qualitative descriptors they applied to the references used in their study. They did not attempt to attribute causal relationships among their findings (Rosales-Dordelly & Short, 1985).

They established the "conceptual framework" and "specialized knowledge" of the field: policy making; development and evaluation; change and enactment, decision making modes; a field of study or an activity; form of inquiry; language for inquiry; and questions directing inquiry. Their knowledge categories were derived within a framework that examined four types of contexts (teaching, program planning, research, consulting), and four descriptors (uniqueness, contemporary relevance, conceptual clarity, subject to criticism). Rosales-Dordelly and Short (1985) concluded that the body of "curriculum knowledge was amphorous, incoherent, and fragmentary." (Rosales-Dordelly & Short, 1985).

Rogan and Luckowski's (1990) investigation analyzed nine of the leading textbooks in the field of curriculum to determine if there were common domains of content knowledge. Their study revealed that there is no dominant textbook in curriculum which establishes a format for other textbooks to follow because there is no consensus on what content knowledge is important for curriculum study. This investigation used domains of content knowledge, a component that is similar to the domains of curriculum used in the study to be described in what follows. However, the domains selected for the Rogan and Luckowski (1990) study and this research study differs in several ways. The criteria for selecting domains of content knowledge in Rogan and Luckowski's (1990) work are not clearly articulated. The authors utilized two criteria for selecting textbooks: (1) books in print published before 1970; and (2) books in authors' estimation to be the most widely used. The domains of curriculum investigated in this study were selected and defined by the investigator's synthesis and research of curriculum textbooks published since 1970.

More recently, Ornstein and Hunkins (1993) concluded that the domains of curriculum, that represent the essential knowledge of the field, varied among both scholars and practitioners. They determined that the technical aspects of curriculum construction, curriculum development, and curriculum design were the only agreed upon and traditional domains.

Up to this point, the constructs dealing with curriculum knowledge and curriculum domains have lacked empirical support. These concepts or ideas were based solely on language and qualitative discussions, not quantifiable data. The fact that there is considerable disagreement about curriculum domains suggests that the field lacks an agreed upon knowledge base.

Domains of Curriculum for this Study

The domains of curriculum for this study were divided into the following eleven areas of study: (1) curriculum philosophy; (2) curriculum theory; (3) curriculum research; (4) curriculum history; (5) curriculum change; (6) curriculum development; (7) curriculum design; (8) curriculum implementation; (9) curriculum evaluation; (10) curriculum policy; and (11) curriculum as a field of study. There were selected using the content analysis procedures of curriculum textbooks published between 1970-1990. The domains of curriculum represent broad conceptualizations of curriculum that describe specific curriculum activities.

One might expect that the teacher groups and the professors would rate and rank the importance of curriculum domains and the related practices similarly. In the same connection, one might also expect that the professors would pick a textbook that advocates the curriculum practices that they identified as being most important, and that there would be a high correlation between their ratings of the importance and their ratings regarding the extent to which these practices were covered in the textbooks they selected. In order to establish a professional knowledge base in curriculum textbooks, a set of collectively agreed upon practices was established for this study.

This study differs from previous research in at least several ways. It was designed to investigate domains of curriculum, hereafter called subscales that have not been examined before. A selected sample chosen from the population of the Professors of Curriculum were participants in an open ended (textbooks) survey and asked to select the most influential textbooks in curriculum. Based on their selection, twelve textbooks were identified. The pool of textbooks identified as most influential was limited to the identification of textbooks published between 1970 and 1990. It is noted that imposing an epochal parameter (i.e., only textbooks published between 1970-1990) for the selection of most influential textbooks will influence the results. Additionally two samples of teacher groups were surveyed and asked to rate the importance of curriculum domains and related practices.

The results of this study should be viewed in the context of the components chosen for the investigation, that is, the domains of curriculum. It is recognized that the selection of a specific component will necessarily influence the results of the study.

Summary

In this chapter, a review of literature related to the conceptual framework of this study was presented. A summary of research that used survey methodology to determine influential curriculum books preceded a discussion of the advantages and disadvantages of textbooks, how textbooks influence learning, and a discussion of the textbook selection and adoption process. A review of research on domains of curriculum and a discussion of literature regarding professional knowledge bases was presented.

CHAPTER III

RESEARCH PROCEDURES

In this chapter, the methodology used in this research study is presented. The chapter is arranged in nine sections covering: (1) the subjects that participated in the study; (2) validity and reliability of the survey instrument; (3) discussion of reliability assessment for the survey; (4) the sample and respondents for the textbook survey; (5) the sample and respondents for the domains survey; (7) overview of parametric and nonparametric statistics; (8) presentation of the procedures used to investigate each research question; and (9) a summary.

Designation of the Sample

Three sample groups participated in this research study, a group of Midwestern urban elementary teachers (N= 48), a group of Southeastern rural elementary teachers (N=37), and the Professors of Curriculum (N =51). The teacher groups were the respondents in a close ended (domains) survey. This survey consisted of a randomized list of 55 statements which described curriculum practices that comprised the domains of curriculum.

The Professors of Curriculum were the respondents for the open ended (textbook) survey and the close ended (domains) survey. These two surveys included the representative list of most influential textbooks and the randomized list of 55 curriculum practices. Elected to membership by invitation, these professors are considered to be the major academicians in the field of curriculum studies. The Professors of Curriculum conduct research and are consultants to schools and education agencies. They often prepare future leaders by teaching courses that are germane to their training. Once again, given their influential role, it seemed desirable to determine the extent of their overall agreement in identifying the most influential curriculum textbooks, their agreement regarding the importance of various curriculum practices and the extent of coverage given to curriculum practices in selected textbooks.

Validity and Reliability of the Survey

Validity

Content validity relates to the test score and all of the factors including clarity of directions and adequacy of scoring procedures that may affect it (Thorndike, Cunningham, Hagen, & Thorndike, 1991). Demonstrating content validity is primarily a subjective process and because the kind of evidence desired depends on the projected use of the results, there is no single agreed-upon way to estimate content validity. Content validity is an inference that is to be made from the test scores derived from the test instrument (Payne, 1974). Content related evidence is not usually stated in numerical form (Ary, Jacobs, & Razavieh, 1990)

The adequacy of content can be assured by defining the universe appropriately and representing the universe fairly in the test. The definitions should include: (1) kinds of tasks, stimuli, or situations over which the universe ranges; (2) kinds of responses that the observer should count; and (3) injunctions to the subject. It is not possible to defend any one universe as correct (Cronbach, 1984). Sampling is best guaranteed by systematically mapping out subdivisions of the universe and collecting the desired number of items for each subdivision (Cronbach, 1984). Critical to content validation is the form of the task itself. A person should not miss scoring an item correctly because of verbal difficulties. Therefore, the form of the items may influence the score (Cronbach, 1984).

To ensure content validity, it is recommended that irrelevant difficulties be excluded. Wherever an example can be simplified without making it a false example, it should be simplified. The task of content validation is to ensure adequate representation of the universe (Cronbach, 1984). Dropping poorly constructed items that are within the same content area might result in reducing the representativeness of the test. The goal of statistical analysis with respect to content validity is to point out ambiguities (Cronbach, 1984).

Examining content validity requires judging whether an item and the distribution of items as a whole covers what the test is reported to measure. This judgment, however, rests more on the test taker than on the author. How close a correspondence should be demanded is subjective (Cronbach, 1984). Content validity is the representativeness or sampling adequacy of the content. It is guided by investigating whether the items of a given test or instrument is representative of the content or the construct that is being measured (Kerlinger, 1987).

Every educational construct has a theoretical universe that consists of all things that can be used to define a construct. The members of the universe, U, are called items (Kerlinger, 1987). The universe for the component domains of curriculum is defined by all of the items listed in each of the categorical subheadings: curriculum philosophy; curriculum theory; curriculum research; curriculum history; curriculum change; curriculum development; curriculum design; curriculum implementation; curriculum evaluation; curriculum policy; and curriculum as a field of study.

It is not possible to completely satisfy the definition of content validity. Content validity relies upon judgment, alone, or with others. In either case, one judges the representativeness of the items (Kerlinger, 1987). The items of a test must be studied and each item must be weighted for its presumed representativeness of the universe. Competent or expect judges should appraise the content of the items. The universe of the content must be clearly defined; judges must be furnished with specific directions for making judgments and specifications of what they are judging. When these procedures are adequate, then it is appropriate to use a method of pooling independent judgments (Kerlinger, 1987).

Popham (1990) recommends two basic strategies that can be applied separately or simultaneously to establish content-related evidence of validity. Expert judges can be called upon to exercise their best judgment in an effort to identify all of the items that represents the universe of a content. This process is refered to as *during test development* (Popham, 1990, p. 98). The second strategy involves subjecting the survey instrument to a series of *post facto judgments* (Ibid., p. 98) about the representativeness of its content. Once again, a panel of expert judges might review the survey item by item, to determine if the items satisfactorily represent the universe of the content that is being measured. For this research study, only the first method, *during test development* (Ibid., p. 98), was used to gather content-related evidence of validity.

Reliability

Reliability can be defined as the consistency of measurement with an evaluation instrument. It provides the consistency that makes validity possible and indicates how much confidence can be placed in the results (Gronlund & Linn, 1990). There are several procedures that can be used to calculate reliability, including alternate form reliability, split-reliability, Kuder-Richardson reliability, and the test-retest reliability (Tuckman, 1988).

A test for reliability was not conducted for the textbook survey instrument. This decision was based on the fact that there existed little likelihood that Professor's of Curriculum responses would be significantly different in one short period of time to necessitate conducting a procedure of this nature or that their responses would be influenced by factors known to effect reliability such as: (1) familiarity with the particular test form; (2) fatigue; (3) emotional strain; (4) physical conditions of the room in which the test is given; (5) health of the test taker; (6) amount of practice or experience by the test taker of a specific skill being measured; (7) fluctuations of human memory; or (8) specific knowledge that has been gained outside of the experience being evaluated by the test (Tuckman, 1988).

While reliability is important, it is not a sufficient condition for validity. It provides the consistency that makes validity possible. Even a high reliability does not insure that a satisfactory degree of validity will exist (Gronlund & Linn, 1990). Conducting a reliability assessment for the textbook survey instrument would have necessitated a larger sample or replication of the survey. Formal reliability assessment was conducted only for the domains survey.

Item analysis procedures are intended to maximize test reliability. Maximization of text reliability is accomplished by determining the relationship between individual items and the text as a whole. It is important to ensure that the overall test is measuring what it is supposed to measure (Thorndike, Cunningham, Hagen, & Thorndike, 1991).

In this study, methods of item analysis were used for the purposes of selecting the best items available for the final survey instrument and highlighting structural or content deficits in the measurement tool (Payne, 1974). There are three main elements in item analysis: (1)

determining the discriminatory power of each item; (2) examining the difficulty level of each item; and (3) in the case of multiple choice or matching question, examining the effectiveness of distractors (Payne, 1974). For the purposes of this study, only the first procedure was considered.

Coefficient alpha (Cronbach's alpha) was used to assess the internal consistency (reliability) of the items examined. Cronbach's alpha is used to compute the internal consistency when measures have multiple scored items or utilize Likert scales and can not be scored as correct or incorrect (Popham, 1990).

If test items are heterogeneous, that is the test items measure more than one construct, then the reliability index computed by coefficient alpha will be lowered. Conversely, if the items are homogeneous, and tend to measure one construct, then the reliability index computed by coefficient alpha will be higher (Ary, Jacobs, & Razavieh, 1990).

Cronbach's alpha is expressed as follows:

$$a \text{ or } r(xx) = \frac{k}{k-1} \frac{(Sx)^2 - (E \text{ Si})^2}{(SX)^2}$$

where K = number of items on the test

$(E \text{ Si})^2$ = sum of the variances of the item scores

$(SX)^2$ = variance of the test scores (all K items)

The variance of all the scores for each item must be determined. Each of these variances across the items will be totaled to get $E(Si)^2$ (Ary, Jacobs, & Razavieh, 1990).

Methods of item analysis yield three statistics for each item, an item discrimination index, the number and/or percentage of respondents marking a choice to each item, (an item mean), and standard deviation. The item discrimination shows the extent to which each item discriminated among the respondents in the same way as the total score discriminates. The item discrimination index is calculated by correlating the item scores with total scale scores (Ary, Jacobs, & Razavieh, 1990).

One way of interpreting the size of the item discrimination index is to eliminate ones with an index below .20 (Thorndike, Cunningham, Hagen, & Thorndike, 1991). Additional support for the selection of this criterion is cited by Payne (1974) and Nunnally (1970). However, other researchers state that each item should correlate at least .25 (Ary, Jacobs, & Razavieh, 1990). The established low end item inclusion cut off score was .20. If an item correlated at less than .20 it was eliminated because that item was not contributing to what the instrument was trying to measure.

The domains and practices were quantified through formal reliability and validity procedures. In phase one of the study, a group of experts (N = 5) independently categorized a list of 89 domain practices into one of eleven domains to help establish content validity. As a result of this categorization process, two curriculum domains (curriculum change and curriculum implementation), were omitted because an insufficient number of curriculum practices were categorized within the domains. Thirty-four domain practices were also omitted as a result of the categorization process.

Alpha correlation coefficients were calculated for each of the curriculum practices and subscales for the domains. By using this procedure, it was possible to identify the degree of agreement: (1) item total correlation between each item and the subscale; and (2) the internal consistency for each subscale, (e.g., the extent of homogeneity of items within a subscale). This procedure permitted the identification of those items that best agreed with each subscale as indicated by the **item-total correlation score.** It also provided evidence related to the degree of internal consistency for each item within a subscale as indicated by the **alpha if item deleted score,** and the degree of internal consistency for each subscale as an entity as indicated by the **alpha correlation coefficient.**

Once, again the curriculum practices were representative of the kinds of activities performed by curriculum specialists (including teachers, principals, coordinators, and directors of curriculum).

For the purposes of establishing reliability, the Midwest teacher group (N =48), the Southeast teachers (N =37) and the Professors of Curriculum group (N=51) each rated the importance of the curriculum practices on a five-point Likert scale from "very important" to "very unimportant" with the midpoint being "of some importance". In order for each curriculum practice to be included in the survey instrument it had to exhibit an item discrimination score of .20 or higher within its respective domain (or subscale) as per the teacher ratings and professor ratings.

Reliability Assessment for the Survey

The item analysis of domain subscales by the Midwestern teachers revealed strong internal consistency with alpha correlation coefficients ranging from .73 to .93. Item-total correlation scores for the curriculum practices by the Midwest were above all .20 which was the established low end item inclusion cut off score. The Southeastern teachers also demonstrated strong internal consistency in their ratings of importance for the domain subscales. The alpha correlation coefficients ranged from .63 to .87. Three practices, one in the domain of curriculum philosophy, one in the domain of curriculum evaluation, and one in the domain of curriculum policy had item-total correlation coefficients were less than .20. These practices were eliminated from the overall analysis. The remaining 52 curriculum practices demonstrated item-total correlation coefficients above .20.

Ratings by the Professors of Curriculum ranged from .62 to .85. Forty-nine curriculum practices had coefficient alphas above .20. The remaining six domain curriculum practices, one in curriculum evaluation, two in curriculum policy, and three in curriculum development had coefficient alphas below .20 and were omitted from further analysis. The reliability data obtained during three separate occasions represents efforts to establish, reassess, and refine the internal consistency of the survey instrument.

The Textbook Survey

Sample

The textbook survey sample consisted of approximately 170 individuals who belonged to a professional organization called the Professors of Curriculum. The sample population for the open ended textbook survey included fifty percent of the 1990-91 Professors of Curriculum membership directory, excluding emeritus professors. The emeritus professors were eliminated from the sample because it was assumed that since they were no longer actively teaching, perhaps they would not be current with respect to the curriculum textbooks published between 1970-1990. An open ended questionnaire was mailed to a selected sample (N = 88) consisting of only those Professors of Curriculum who were currently affiliated with a college or university. (See Appendix A).

Responses

Forty-seven responses were received from the professors, yielding a 53% return from the sample population for the open ended survey. Taken together, the respondents cited a total of 280 books. The mean number of books selected by each respondent, irrespective of sex groups was 7.58 textbooks.

Of the 47 professors who responded to the open ended survey, nine declined to list books for reasons listed below: four because they felt unqualified to do so; two because of a tight traveling schedule; two because they didn't feel any textbooks had impacted the field of curriculum; and one because of retirement. Professors who declined to list books constituted 19.14% of the returned surveys and represented 10.23% of the sample population who were contacted to participate in the open ended survey. These incomplete surveys were excluded from further analysis. The remaining 38 surveys, 43.2% of the original sample population, comprised the final data set that was statistically analyzed.

The Domains Survey

Sample

The sample for the domains survey included all of the Professors of Curriculum in the U.S. and Canada who were actively teaching and conducting research (N=132). As previously described, thirty-four of the members of the one hundred and sixty-six Professors of Curriculum were retired and since they were emeritus, they were omitted from the sample survey for reasons already discussed.

The respondents were instructed to select the one textbook with which they were most familiar, rate the importance of the curriculum practices (or items) based on their opinion, and to rate the extent to which each curriculum practice (or item) was covered within the textbook they selected.

The domains survey was used for the second portion of the data collection and mailed to the urban elementary Midwest teacher group, the rural elementary Southeast teacher group, and all of the Professors of Curriculum who were affiliated with a college or university teaching (N = 132). (Refer to Appendices B and C).

Responses

Eighty-six (86) responses or 65.15% were received from the Professors of Curriculum. Overall, fifty-one (51) of the respondents, that is, 38.64% of the sample population, completed the survey. Several respondents, N = 35 or 26.52%, returned the survey and declined to complete it for one of the reasons shown below:

1.	Retired	N = 6
2.	Didn't feel qualified	N = 6
3.	Didn't care to participate	N = 6
4.	Didn't agree with the survey	N = 4
5.	Didn't respond to these type of research studies	N = 3
6.	Health prohibited participation	N = 3
7.	Didn't agree with textbook selections	N = 3
8.	Unable to locate respondent due to travel	N = 3
9.	Respondent is deceased	N = 1

Four respondents disagreed with the survey. Of the three respondents who disagred with the textbook selection, two stated that they had not used any of the books listed in the survey. Six professors declined to complete the survey on the basis of a lack of grounding in the basic textbooks, indicating that they didn't feel qualified to respond. Perhaps this says something about the nature of the field, and/or this finding may have implications about who gets elected to the Professors of Curriculum. Six professors indicated they were retired, three declined to participate for health reasons, and one professor was reported to be deceased. Professors who declined to participate beacuse they lacked expertise, were retired, or were unable to participate due to health, death, or travel totaled 19, and represented 14.39% of the sample population (N = 132). Those that either disagreed with the textbook selection, or the survey, totaled 7, or 5.3% of the sample population   (N = 132).

Parametric and Nonparametric Statistics

This section describes the conditions which determine the application of parametric and nonparametric statistics. It concludes with a rationale for selecting nonparametric methods.

Using parametric statistical tests depends upon a number of assumptions about the population from which the sample used in the study is drawn. There are no assumptions as to the forms of the sample population or the values of the population parameters for using nonparametric or distribution free statistical tests. In order to use **parametric** tests, the following conditions must be satisfied.

(1) The normally assumption cannot be vitiated, that is, the sample from which data is drawn must be normally distributed (Kerlinger, 1987). When in doubt about the normality of the population, nonparametric tests should be used.

(2) Homogeneity of variance must be present. In analysis of variance, the variances within the groups must be statistically the same, that is homogeneous from group to group within the bounds of random variation (Kerlinger, 1987). Unless there is good evidence to believe populations are seriously non normal and that variances are heterogeneous, it is unwise to use a nonparametric test in place of a parametric one.

(3) Measures to be analyzed need to be continuous with equal intervals (Kerlinger, 1987).

(4) Independence of observations or statistical independence must exist. In research, it is assumed that observations are independent and that making one observation does influence the making of another observation. This assumption applies no matter what kind of statistical test is used, because violating it invalidates the results of most statistical tests of significance (Kerlinger, 1987).

Nonparametric tests should be implemented when the following conditions are satisfied.

(1) When the sample size is small, there may be no applicable parametric statistical procedure. Unless the nature of the population distribution is known exactly, nonparametric methods should be used (Siegel, 1988).

(2) Nonparametric tests make fewer assumptions about the data and may be more appropriate for a particular situation. A hypothesis test by nonparametric methodology may be more suitable for the research investigation (Siegel, 1988).

(3) Data that are inherently measured in ranks, can be categorized as plus or minus (more or less, better or worse), and who numerical scores have the strength of ranks should be analyzed by nonparametric tests (Siegel, 1988).

(4) Nonparametric procedures are available to analyze data which are categorical such as nominal data. There are no parametric techniques available that apply to such data (Siegel, 1988).

(5) Nonparametric statistical tests can be implemented to treat samples made up of observations from several different populations. Parametric techniques typically can not handle data without requiring unrealistic assumptions or cumbersome computations (Siegel, 1988).

For this investigation, the normality assumption is not in doubt. The homogeneity of variance in not in question either. The variances within groups do not differ so widely that averaging becomes questionable. The effect of widely differing variances would result in inflating the within groups variance. The measures to be analyzed are continuous measures with equal intervals. All of the measure are statistically independent.

The data for research question one is descriptive. There are no statistical procedures to test the veracity or falsity of research question number 1. The data for research question 2 is categorical and nominal. There are no parametric tests available to assess nominal data. The data sets for research questions 3, 4, and 5 are ordinal and are tabulated as frequencies. The numerical scores have the strengths of ranks. Given the ordinal data sets used in this investigation, nonparametric rather than parametric procedures are the appropriate statistical tests to use for data analysis.

For the purposes of rating the importance and the extent of text coverage given to the items within the domains of curriculum, the Likert scale, a method of summated ratings, was chosen. Five response categories were utilized so that the weighing of both scales were equal. The statements in the questionnaire were arranged in random order so as to avoid any possibility of a response set on the part of the professors (Ary, Jacobs, & Razavieh, 1990). The items listed in the domains subscales were taken from the content of the definitions section. All of the items in each domains subscale were assumed to be of equal weight for the purposes of this study.

Research Question Procedures

Research procedures are conducted in order to make statistical inferences about testing hypotheses. They are a tool for the advancement of knowledge and help the investigator confirm or disconfirm hypotheses (Kerlinger, 1987). Procedures of statistical inference suggest some of the necessary conditions for data collection and determine whether the investigator can have confidence in conclusions drawn from the data (Siegel, 1988). The following is a description of the procedures used to address each of the research questions.

Procedures for Research Question 1

Using an open ended survey approach, the Professors of Curriculum (N=88) were asked to simply list textbooks published between 1970-1990 which they believed have had the most impact in the field of curriculum. (Refer to Appendix A). The respondents were asked to list up to ten textbooks without indicating any kind of rank order. Those books selected in the top twelve rankings from the total pool of open ended responses were listed as the most influential textbooks for the close ended (domains) survey that was distributed to the Professors of Curriculum (See Table 4.1, pp. 50, 51). The textbooks selected were ranked according to frequency of response given for each textbook cited.

Because the assumption of normality was invalidated and the data to be analyzed did not constitute continuous measures with equal intervals, measuring agreement could not be statistically defined. The selection of the most influential textbooks could not be correlated nor could it be ranked either parametrically or nonparametrically.

Descriptive statistics were used to assess the results. The frequency of textbook selections was described in terms of percentages. After the frequencies were tallied, textbook selections were also rank ordered. The mean number of books cited by each respondent was calculated.

The original criterion for selecting a textbook as most influential was designated as 20%. Eight textbooks met this criterion. However, four textbooks were cited by 15.8% and tied for rank order ten. Since the survey directions asked the professors to list up to ten textbooks, it seemed necessary to establish a list of at least ten influential textbooks. By extending this list to 12 books, there was a greater likelihood that the Professors of Curriculum would see one book that they were most familiar with and increase their inclination to respond to the survey.

It should be noted that textbook authors were not necessarily omitted from the sample population for the textbook (open ended) survey. However, textbook authors who participated in the open ended (textbook) survey constituted only 5.7% of the sample populations. It is interesting to note that one author who participated did not list his own work as one of the most influential textbooks. Four of the textbooks in Table 4.1 (See pp. 50, 51) were cited by their author. Seven of the authors cited in Table 4.1 were not participants in the open ended survey. However, it should be noted that a book could only be cited once by any given respondent. In actuality, only 5 of the 12 textbook authors listed in Table 4.1 were respondents in the open ended survey.

Procedures for Research Question 2

Using the mainframe version of SPSS-X and Nonpar Tests, the Crosstabs, and Frequency programs were implemented to run Chi-square statistics and the Kolmogorov-Smirnov test for two independent samples to assess the potential of significant relationships between the demographic variables and the professors' textbook selection and to determine the influence of demographic variables by textbook selections (Ary, Jacobs, & Razavieh, 1990, and SPSS-X, 1988).

Chi-square statistics were computed to assess the potential of significance differences in responses related to the selection of the twelve most influential curriculum textbooks across: a) gender; b) doctorate specialization (curriculum and/or instruction) or other); c) year (in ten year intervals) doctorate was earned; d) geographical region of the institution (Northwest, Northeast, Southwest, Southeast, or Midwest), where the doctorate was awarded; and e) geographical region of the professors' current institutional affiliation (Northwest, Northeast, Southwest, Southeast, or Midwest), (SPSS-X, 1988).

When calculating Chi-square statistics using 2 by 2 contingency tables, it is necessary that the occurrence of cell frequencies with values less than five not exceed 20% of the total number of cells. Because of the small number of frequencies within cells, it was necessary to collapse categories within variables. The geographical region of the institution where the doctorate was awarded and the Professors of Curriculum current institutional affiliation was collapsed into two categories. The Northeast and Southeast were designated as East or category l; the Midwest was designated as category 2. Since, none of the professors earned their degree at institutions located in the Northwest or Southwest the categories were not included in the analysis.

In reference to the Professors of Curriculum current institutional affiliation, the data for the Northwest, Southwest, and Midwest were combined into category 1, designated as West. Northeast and Southeast were collapsed into category 2, or East.

The year in which the doctorate was awarded was originally coded into six categories: Before 1941; 1941-1950; 1951-1960; 1961-1970; 1971-1980; and 1981-1990. None of the respondents received their doctorates prior to 1951. Data for this variable was collapsed into two categories. Individuals receiving their doctorate between 1951 and 1970 were recoded as category one. Those receiving doctorates between 1971 to 1990 were recoded into category 2.

Chi-Square Test

The Chi-square test of independence was employed to find the significance of differences between males and females in their selection of each of the twelve most influential textbooks. The Chi-square statistic was used because the following criteria were met: (1) observations were independent; subjects were randomly and independently selected; (2) the categories were mutually exclusive; and (3) the observations were measured as frequencies.

The Frequency program was utilized to count and record the percentages of males and females who chose the most influential curriculum textbooks, to indicate how many individuals received their doctorates in curriculum and instruction as opposed to another field in education, to reveal what year Professors of Curriculum earned their doctorates, and to demonstrate how many professors received their doctorates at institutions located in the East and the Midwest, and the regional location of the institutions where the professors were currently teaching West (including the Midwest) and East (SPSS-X, 1988). Two by two contingency tables were computed for each analysis. In addition, Pearson and the phi statistics were calculated for each analysis.

Kolmogorov-Smirnov Test

The Nonpar Tests were implemented in order to utilize the Kolmogorov-Smirnov (K-S) two sample test subcommand. The K-S two sample test is a measure of whether two independent samples have been drawn from the same population. The maximum positive, negative, and absolute differences in relationship to the professors' gender, doctorate specialization, year the doctorate was earned, geographical region where the doctorate was earned, and the geographical region of the current institutional affiliation, the K-S (Z), and a two-tailed level of probability (p) was computed for each test. The 2 tailed test detected any kind of differences within the distribution from which the two samples were drawn.

The K-S test is concerned with agreement between the distribution of a set of sample values and some specified theoretical distribution. If two samples have been chosen from the same population distribution, then the cumulative frequency distribution of both samples may be expected to be fairly close, devoid of any large deviations in the cumulative frequency distributions between the two samples. If a large deviation between the two sample cumulative frequency distributions are demonstrated, it suggests that the samples are drawn from two different populations. A large enough deviation between the two sample cumulative frequency distributions is evidence for rejecting the null hypothesis (Siegel, 1988).

With respect to research question 2, this procedure determined the potential level of disagreement among the Professors' of Curriculum selection of the most influential textbooks across the aforementioned demographic variables. A K-S (Z) value of zero indicated total agreement and a non significant relationship among the professors in their selection of the most influential curriculum textbooks in relationship to the variables under investigation. A K-S (Z) value that was positive or negative demonstrated disagreement. The observed deviation would have to be large enough to result in statistical significance.

Procedures for Research Questions 3 and 4

The following procedures describe the scoring and weightings of items in the close ended domains survey for research questions 3 and 4. For the purposes of statistical analysis, items in the domains of curriculum were assumed to be of equal weight.

Each of the domains, (curriculum philosophy, curriculum theory, curriculum research, curriculum history, curriculum development, curriculum design, curriculum evaluation, curriculum policy, and curriculum as a field of study) were represented by four or more items. Once again, curriculum change and curriculum implementation were eliminated by expert judges during the development of the test due to an insufficient number of representative items. The domains were not identified by name and the items of each domain were intermixed. The domains survey was mailed to an urban sample of Midwestern elementary teachers and a rural sample of Southeastern elementary teachers. The teacher groups were asked to rate importance of items (curriculum practices) within the domains of curriculum without knowing which items fell within specific subscales using a five point Likert rating scale ([5] very important, [4] fairly important, [3] some importance, [2] fairly unimportant, [1] very unimportant). (Refer to Appendix B).

Procedures for Research Question 5

The same procedures that were used to assess the ratings of importance of the items within the domains of curriculum for research questions three and four were also implemented to assess the Professors of Curriculum ratings of importance for research question five. As previously described, the survey listed 55 items that comprised nine domains of curriculum.

Additionally, the professors were given the list of twelve textbooks identified as being the most influential in the textbook portion of the survey. In the closed ended domains survey, they were instructed to select one textbook with which they were most familiar and asked to rate the extent to which each of the items was covered within the textbook they selected. A five point Likert rating scale was used ([5] very great extent, [4] great extent, [3] some extent, [2] little extent, [1] very little extent). Subscales for the domains of curriculum were calculated for use in other statistical analysis. (Refer to Appendix C).

Re-Assessing reliability

As a further test of reliability, Cronbach's alpha was calculated for each respondent's score for the ratings of the importance of curriculum practices within the domains of curriculum (subscales) and the ratings of the extent to which the curriculum practices within the domains of curriculum were covered within the textbook that the Professors of Curriculum selected (SPSS-X, 1988). By using this procedure, it was possible to identify the degree of agreement, item-total correlation between each item and the subscale, as well as the internal consistency for each subscale, that is the extent of homogeneity within subscale.

Once again, this procedure also identified those items that best agreed with each subscale as indicated by the **item-total correlation score**, the degree of internal consistency for each item within subscale as indicated by the **alpha if item deleted score** and the degree of internal consistency for each subscale as an entity as indicated by the **alpha correlation coefficient.** This particular test did not analyze the textbook chosen by the participants in relationship to the correlation coefficient being calculated.

The low end item inclusion cut off score was .20. The rationale for establishing the item cut off score at .20 was for the following reasons:

l) to prevent the lost of too many curriculum practices; 2) to prevent diminishing the contribution of subscales to the overall meaning of the instrument (Cronbach, 1984); and 3) because using .20 as a low end item inclusion cut off score was supported in the literature (Thorndike, Cunningham, Hagen, & Thorndike, 1991; Payne, 1974; Nunnally, 1970). However, by deleting items with insufficient alpha coefficients the overall reliability of the respective subscales increased.

Spearman rho correlation measures

To assess the extent of agreement between the professors' ratings of importance and coverage, the SPSS-X program Nonpar Corr was used to compute Spearman rho correlation coefficients. A (p) value was calculated for each of the subscales under the domains of curriculum. The textbooks selected were not considered to be items for analysis in the Nonpar Corr test (Ary, Jacobs, & Razavieh, 1990).

The Spearman rank-order correlation coefficient is a measure association between two variables that ranks objectives or individuals into two series. This procedure requires that both variables be measured in ordinal scales. The Spearman rank order correlation coefficient was used to rank the responses of the respondents on their rankings of importance (X_i) for each of the items within the nine subscales listed under the domains of curriculum and compare their relationship to the rankings of the ratings of the extent to which all of the items within the subscales were covered (Y_i) with textbooks. If the ratings were perfect $X_i=Y_i$ each person would have the same rankings on the data pairs of each subscale.

$D_i=X_i - Y_i$ indicates the disparity between the two sets of rankings. Since the researcher was interested in the total magnitude of the disparity between the rankings, rather than the sign (positive or negative) of all the differences between the rankings of the two variables importance and coverage D_i^2 was employed so that the index of disparity was displayed as the total magnitude. The value of ED_i^2 is the sum of squared differences for the N pairs of data.

The formula for the Spearman rank-order correlation coefficient is:

$$r(s) = \frac{(EXi)^2 + (EYi)^2 - (EDi)^2}{2\,(EXi)^2\,(EYi)^2}$$

where r(s) = ranks

$(EXi)^2$ = sum of the squared scores for variable Xi

$(EYi)^2$ = sum of the squared scores for variable Yi

$(EDi)^2$ = sum of the squared differences between Xi-Yi

and

$$r(s) = \frac{1 - 6\,(EDi)^2}{N3 - N}$$

where

N = the number of pairs of data.

The Spearman rho correlation was utilized to measure the degree of association of importance of items and the extent to which items within the domains (subscales) of curriculum were covered in the most influential textbooks. For each domain (subscale), the scores for all the items were totaled and divided by the number of items within the domain. A correlation of zero indicated a level of perfect disagreement between the rankings of importance and the ratings of the extent to which items within the categories were covered within the most influential curriculum textbooks. The value of (p) would demonstrate a non significant relationship.

For this study, a correlation of + or -.25 to .50 would reveal an acceptable correlation, but a small degree of agreement between the rankings of importance and the extent to which items within the domains were covered within the most influential textbooks. The value of (p) would demonstrate that agreement between importance and coverage did exist. A correlation of + or -.50 to .75 was considered a mid-range correlation. Correlations of + or -.75 to 1.00 were considered high correlations.

Since the Professors of Curriculum were given the option to freely choose one of the twelve textbooks identified as being the most influential, the assumption of normality was invalidated and the data to be analyzed did not constitute continuous measures with equal intervals. With respect to the textbooks, it was not possible to correlate the results of ratings of the extent to which the most important curriculum practices within the domains of curriculum were covered by using either parametric or nonparametric methods. Therefore, the results regarding the textbooks were assessed by using qualitative methods. Frequency of textbook selection was cited. Descriptive statistics were used to discuss the results of the rankings of the degree to which items were covered within the various textbooks. The procedures described were used to assess the importance of the curriculum practices and the extent to which curriculum practices within the domains of curriculum.

Summary

This chapter presented a description of the respondents who participated in the open ended (textbook) and the domains surveys, a discussion of formal procedures that were used to establish validity and reliability, an overview of parametric and nonparametric statistics, and a rationale for selecting nonparametric techniques. The final portion of this chapter provided an explication of the procedures that were implemented to investigate each of the research questions.

CHAPTER IV

ANALYSIS OF DATA

Once again, the overall purpose of this research study was to establish a quantifiable knowledge base of domains and related curriculum practices and identify the most influential textbooks in the field of curriculum. This chapter presents the findings and an analysis of the data sets related to each of the research questions. First, an analysis of the data set regarding the textbook survey will be presented. Then, an analysis of the data sets regarding the domains survey will be presented in an attempt to address each of the remaining research questions of interest.

Results Related to Research Question 1

Forty-seven responses, yielding a 53% return were received. The professors cited a listed a total of 280 books. The mean number of books selected by each respondent, irrespective of sex groups was 7.58 textbooks. Table 4.1 lists these books and the number of votes that each received in rank order, the publisher, and publication date.

Table 4.1

The Most Influential Textbooks in Curriculum in Order of Rank Selected by the Professors of Curriculum.

<u>Author</u>	<u>Textbook Title</u>		
<u>Votes</u> <u>Percent</u>	<u>Rank</u>		
<u>Publisher</u>		<u>Publication Date</u>	
Schubert, W.	*Curriculum: Perspectives, Paradigm, and Possibility*		
25 65.8	1		
Macmillan		1986	
Eisner, E.	*The Educational Imagination*		
23 60.5	2		
Macmillan		1985	
Tanner, D. &	*Curriculum Development: Theory into*		
Tanner, L.	*Practice*		
20 52.6	3		
Macmillan		1980	
Zais, R.	*Curriculum: Principles and Foundations*		
12 31.6	4		
Crowell		1976	
Eisner, E. &	*Conflicting Conceptions of*		
Vallance, E.	*Curriculum*		
11 28.9	5.5		
McCutchan		1974	
Pinar, W.	*Curriculum Theorizing: The*		
	Reconceptualists		
11 28.9	5.5		
McCutchan		1975	
Apple, M.	*Ideology and Curriculum*		
9 23.7	7		
Routledge & Paul		1986	

Table 4.1 contd

Author	Textbook Title		
Votes Percent	Rank		
Publisher	Publication Date		

Kliebard, H.   *The Struggle for the American*
                   Curriculum (1983-1958)
8   21.1   8
Routledge & Paul   1986

Giroux, H.,
Penna A.,
& Pinar, W.   *Curriculum and Instruction*
6   15.8   10
McCutchan   1981

Goodlad, J.   *A Place Called School*
6   15.8   10
McGraw Hill   1984

Goodlad, J.   *Curriculum Inquiry*
6   15.8   10
McGraw   Hill   1979

Pinar, W.   *Contemporary Curriculum*
                   Discourses
6   15.8   10
Gorsuch & Scarisbrick   1988

An examination of Table 4.1 indicates that there was considerable agreement in the rankings among the Professors of Curriculum with respect to their ratings of the most influential textbooks. [1,2]

Schubert's, Eisner's and Tanner and Tanner's textbooks were ranked one, two, and three respectively. Schubert's *Curriculum: Perspectives, Paradigm, and Possibility* received 25 votes and was cited by 65.8% of the respondents; Eisner's *The Educational Imagination* received 23 votes and was selected by 60.5% of the respondents; Tanner and Tanner's *Curriculum Development: Theory into Practice* received 20 votes and was cited by 52.6% of the respondents. Zais' *Curriculum: Principles and Foundations* earned 12 votes by 31.6% of the respondents. Eisner and Vallance's *Conflicting Conceptions of Curriculum* and Pinar's *Curriculum Theorizing: The Reconceptualists* both were given 11 votes by 28.9% of the respondents. Apple's *Ideology and Curriculum* earned 9 votes by 21.1% of the respondents.

Table 4.2
Number of Respondents by Demographic Variable in Percentages for the Textbook Survey

---

DEMOGRAPHIC VARIABLE

GENDER	M = 71.1% (27) * F = 29.9%(11)

YRDEG (1)	1951-60 = 10.5%(4)	1961-70 = 42.18%(16)
	1971-80 = 34.2%(13)	1981-90 = 13.2%(5)

LOCDEG (2)	NE** = 39.5%(15)	MW*** = 39.5%(15)
	SE+ = 21.1%(8)	

LOCINS (3)   NE = 18.4%(7)   MW = 26.3%(10)
                 SE = 34.2%(13)   NW++ =5.3%(2)
                 SW+++ = 15.8%(6)

DEGRE (4)	C & I*+ = 89.5% (4)	OTHER = 10.5%(4)

Notes: 1 = Year doctoral degree awarded
         2 = geographical region of institution where doctorate was awarded
         3 = geographical region of institution of current affiliation
         4 = major field of doctoral study
         * = Actual number of respondents   ** = Northeast
         *** = Midwest   + = Southeast
         ++ = Northwest   +++ = Southwest
         *+ = Curriculum and Instruction

As shown in Table 4.2, descriptive statistics indicated that the sample was comprised of 71.1 % or N = 27 males (M), and 29.9% or N = 11 females (F). Demographic data revealed that four individuals or 10.5% received their doctorate between 1951-1960. YRDEG shows that most of the respondents, that is 42.18% or (N=16) completed their doctorate between 1961-1970. Thirteen individuals or 34.2% earned their doctorate between 1971-1980. Between 1981-1990, 13.2% of (N = 5) earned their doctorate. None of the respondents were awarded their doctorate before 1950.

Those receiving doctorates at institutions (LOCDEG) in both the Northeast (NE) and Midwest (MW) were found to be equal (N = 15 or 39.5%). Eight individuals or 21.1 % were awarded the doctorate at institutions located in the Southeast (SE). None of the respondents completed doctorates at institutions located in the Northwest or Southwest.

Ten respondents or 26.3% were actively teaching in institutions (LOCINS) located in the Midwest (MW), 13 or 34.2% in the Southeast (SE), 7 or 18.4% in the Northeast (NE) or 6 in the Southwest (SW) or (15.8%), and 2 in the Northwest (NW) or (5.3%).

Thirty-four or 89.5% of the respondents had a degree in curriculum and/or instruction (C & I). Four individuals or 10.5% had a doctorate in another field of study (OTHER).

Overall, the sample was comprised of mostly male, curriculum and instruction professors who completed their doctorates between 1961 and 1980 at Eastern or Midwestern and Western universities. The majority of respondents, 20 professors, indicated that they taught at Eastern universities.

Results Related to Research Question 2

Evaluating Significant Relationships

Chi-square statistics were used to evaluate the potential of a significant relationship between textbooks and the aforementioned demographic variables and partially address the following questions.
1. Was there was a significant difference in the rankings among the Professors of Curriculum in their ratings of the most influential textbooks and their gender?
2. Was there a significant difference in the rankings among the Professors of Curriculum in their ratings of the most influential textbooks and their doctorate specialization?

3. Was there a significant difference in the rankings among the Professors of Curriculum in their ratings of the most influential textbooks and the geographical region of their current affiliation?

4. Was there a significant difference in the rankings among the Professors of Curriculum in their ratings of the most influential textbooks and the geographical region of the institution where they received their doctorate?

5. Was there a significant difference in the rankings among the Professors of Curriculum in their ratings of the most influential textbooks and the year they earned their doctorate?

Table 4.3

Summary of Pearson and Phi Statistics for Professors of Curriculum Selection of Textbooks vs. Demographic Variable

DEMOGRAPHIC VARIABLE	Pearson	Phi statistic
Gender	.78	.78
Doctorate specialization	.30	.30
Year doctorate was earned	.32	.32
Geographical region of institution where doctorate was earned	.08	.08
Geographical region of current affiliation	.54	.54

The same complement of 27 (71.1%) males and 11 (28.9%) females was used to assess the potential of significant relationships. Table 4.3 shows the Pearson and phi statistics for each demographic variable.

An assessment of the potential of significant relationships among females and males' rankings in their rating of the most influential textbooks in the field of curriculum revealed both a non significant

Pearson and the phi statistic of .78. This means that gender did not significantly influence the selection of the most influential textbooks.

In analyzing the potential of significant relationships among the professors' doctorate specialization (curriculum and/or instruction or other) in relationship in their rankings of the most influential textbooks, their responses revealed both a non significant Pearson and phi statistic of .30. The professors' doctorate specialization did not appear to significantly influence the selection of the most influential curriculum textbooks.

Assessing the relationship between the year the professors earned their doctorate with respect to their rankings of the ratings of the most influential textbooks evidenced both non significant Pearson and phi statistic of .32.[3] The results demonstrate that the year in which professors earned their doctorates did not significantly influence the selection of the most influential textbooks.

Analyzing the potential of a significant relationship between the geographical region of the institution where the doctorate was earned with respect to the rankings of the most influential textbooks demonstrated both a non significant Pearson and phi statistic of .08.[4] The results indicate that where professors earned their doctorates did not significantly influence their selection of the most influential textbooks.

In assessing the relationship between the geographical region of the Professors of Curriculum current affiliation and their ranking of the ratings of the most influential textbooks, the Pearson and the phi statistical values were found to be non significant. The findings demonstrate that the geographical region of the Professors of Curriculum current affiliation did not significantly influence the professors of rankings of the ratings of the most influential textbooks.

The results demonstrate that non significant Pearson and phi statistics were evidenced for each of the demographic variables. The findings revealed that there were no significant differences in rankings among the Professors of Curriculum in their ratings of the most influential textbooks by: a) genders; b) doctorate specializations; c) year doctorate was earned; d) geographical region of the institution where the doctorate was earned; and e) the geographical region of their current institutional affiliation.

Assessing Agreement

The Kolmogorov-Smirnov two-sample test was implemented in an effort to assess the level of agreement between the Professors of Curriculum selection of textbooks and demographic variables, and determine whether there were significant differences in the rankings among the professors in their ratings of the most influential textbooks across the aforementioned demographic variables.

The SPSS-X Nonpar Corr program was implemented in order to utilize the Kolmogorov-Smirnov two-sample test. The following research questions were addressed using the Kolmogorov-Smirnov test in an effort to assess the level of agreement between the Professors of Curriculum selection of textbooks and the demographic variables. Were there significant differences in rankings among the Professors of Curriculum in their ratings of the most influential textbooks across: a) gender; b) doctorate specialization; c) year doctorate was earned; d) geographical region of the institution where the doctorate was earned; or e) the geographical region of their current institutional affiliation?

Table 4.4

Summary of Results of the K-S Two-Sample Test of Agreement for the Professors of Curriculum Selection of Textbooks by Demographic Variables

DEMOGRAPHIC VARIABLE		
	K-S value	p level
Gender	.377	<.999
Doctorate specialization	.250	<1.00
Year Doctorate was earned	.445	<.989
Geographical region where the doctorate was earned	.821	<.510
Geographical region of current institutional affiliation	.274	<1.00

Table 4.4 shows the results of the K-S test. The results demonstrated non significant p values for each of the aforementioned questions. The probability levels related to each of the demographic variables were < .999, 1.00, <.989, <.510, and 1.00 respectively.

In analyzing the level of agreement between the professors' textbook selection and gender, the results demonstrated a K-S value of .377 and p ≤ .999. This indicated that both samples were homogeneous groups.

Curriculum and/or instruction and doctorate specialization in another field were the samples that were used in the analysis to assess the level of agreement between the professors' textbook selections and doctorate specialization. A K-S value of .250 and p ≤ 1.000 revealed that both samples were homogeneous.

The period of 1951 to 1970 and 1971 to 1990 were the two samples used to analyze the level of agreement between the professor's textbook selection and the year the doctorate was earned. A K-S value of .445 and p ≤ .989 indicated that both samples were homogeneous.

Regions designated as the Midwest and the East were the two samples utilized to investigate the level of agreement between the professors' textbook selections and the geographical region where the professors earned their doctorates. A K-S value of .821 and a p ≤ .510 provided evidence that both samples were homogeneous.

West, including the Midwest and East constituted the two samples analyzed to determine the level of agreement between the professors' textbook selection and the geographical region of their current affiliation. A K-S value of .274, and p ≤ 1.000 demonstrated that both samples were homogeneous.

An overview of the K-S results demonstrated several high probability scores. It is notable that the resulting p values for determining the level of agreement between the Professors of Curriculum selection of the most influential curriculum textbooks and doctorate specialization, and the Professors of Curriculum selection of the most influential textbooks and year they earned their doctorate yielded a very high probability score of ≤ 1.00.

Assessing the level of agreement between the Professors of Curriculum identification of the most influential textbooks and gender evidenced a high probability score at the ≤ .999 level. Determining the level of agreement between the Professors of Curriculum selection of the most influential textbooks and the geographical region of their current affiliation resulted in a high probability score at the ≤ .989 level. The level of agreement between the Professors of Curriculum selection of the most influential textbooks and the geographical region of the institution at which the doctorate was earned demonstrated a probability score in the mid-high range at the $\leq$ .510 level (Refer to Table 4.4).

Taken as a whole, the results of the K-S test demonstrate that there were no significant differences among the Professors of Curriculum in their ratings of the most influential textbooks by gender, doctorate specialization, year doctorate was earned, geographical region of the institution where the doctorate was earned, and the geographical region of their current institutional affiliation. Finally, it should be noted that the findings related to the K-S test demonstrate that the two samples analyzed for all five comparisons were taken from the same population and were homogeneous groups.

Results Related to Research
Questions 3 and 4

Table 4.5

Item-Total Correlations and Alpha Coefficients for the Importance of Curriculum Practices within the Domains of Curriculum by the Midwest Teacher Group (*MWTCHR*), Southeast Teacher Group (*SETCHR*), and the Professors of Curriculum (*PROFCURR*).

DOMAINS OF CURRICULUM

ITEM-TOTAL CORRELATIONS

MWTCHR	SETCHR	PROFCURR
(N = 48)	(N = 37)	(N = 51)

I. CURRICULUM PHILOSOPHY

a=.7307*	a=.6435*	a=.8450*

Curriculum Practice

1. Reflecting upon schools of thought including: perennialism; essentialism; progressivism; reconstructionism; and existentialism.

.2660	.3206	.7025

2. Determines the ends of education.

.3748	c	.4880

3. Determines an orientation to curriculum.

.4228	.2925	.6799

4. Suggests a view of society and students. in relationship to education.

.4873	.5286	.5323

5. States the purposes of education.

.6670	.4926	.6428

6. Elaborates on the theory of curriculum.

.6337	.3200	.7101

Table 4.5 contd

ITEM-TOTAL CORRELATIONS

MWTCHR	SETCHR	PROFCURR
(N = 48)	(N = 37)	(N=51)

II. CURRICULUM THEORY

a=.8306	a=.6950	a=.6974

Curriculum Practice

7. Creates statements that give meaning to a school curriculum.

.5470	.4916	.6467

8. Uses techniques of science and logic to present a systematic view of phenomena.

.6930	.5410	.4298

9. Deals with structuring knowledge.

.6202	.4442	.4969

10. Identifies how students learn.

.6509	.5722	.4237

11. Uses principles and rules to study curriculum.

.6393	.2364	.2630

Table 4.5 contd
ITEM-TOTAL CORRELATIONS

MWTCHR	SETCHR	PROFCURR
(N = 48)	(N = 37)	(N = 51)

III. CURRICULUM RESEARCH
a=.8468   a=.6920   a=.7340

Curriculum Practice

12. Analyzes resisting and supporting forces.
.7320   .3308   .4059

13. Advances hypotheses and assumptions of the field.
.6502   .4699   .5783

14. Uses systematic inquiry for the purpose of solving a particular problem.
.7192   .5804   .4473

15. Analyzes steps to be taken in problem solving.
.5778   .4269   .5201

16. Focuses on research and/or inquiry of curriculum.
.5993   .4307   .5243

IV. CURRICULUM HISTORY
a=.7884   a=.6473   a=.7580

Curriculum Practice
17. Describes past curriculum thought and practices.
.6290   .4591   .4127

18. Interprets past curriculum practice.
.6500   .4598   .7323

19. Provides a chronology of important events in curriculum.
.5052   .3370   .5725

20. Examines forces that inhibit curriculum innovations.
.5932   .4639   .2322

Table 4.5 contd

ITEM-TOTAL CORRELATIONS

MWTCHR (N = 48)	SETCHR (N = 37)	PROFCURR (N = 51)

V. CURRICULUM DEVELOPMENT

a=.8695	a=.7278	a=.6236

<u>Curriculum Practice</u>

21. Develops curriculum guides.

.7951	.3678	b

22. Develops school grants.

.7046	.4610	b

23. Determines procedures necessary for a curriculum plan.

.7317	.3120	.1988

24. Addresses questions of who will be involved in curriculum construction.

.5622	.5834	b

25. Integrates content and learning experiences.

.5797	.6075	.4917

26. Decides on nature and organization of curriculum.

.6551	.4889	.6499

Table 4.5 contd

ITEM-TOTAL CORRELATIONS

MWTCHR	SETCHR	PROFCURR
(N = 48)	(N = 37)	(N = 51)

VI. CURRICULUM DESIGN

a=.9049	a=.8663	a=.8505

Curriculum Practice

27. Attempts to define what subject matter will be used.

.5282	.4894	.6288

28. Guides program development for individual students.

.7200	.4639	.7463

29. Selects subject matter and learning experiences.

.7408	.7088	.6173

30. Establishes the primary focus of subject matter.

.8568	.8427	.7389

31. Permits curriculum ideas to function.

.6524	.6025	.4871

32. Integrates careful planning.

.7818	.6624	.7631

33. Indicates instructional strategies to be utilized.

.7830	.7116	.3492

Table 4.5 contd

ITEM-TOTAL CORRELATIONS

MWTCHR	SETCHR	PROFCURR
(N = 48)	(N = 37)	(N = 51)

VII. CURRICULUM EVALUATION
a=.9332   a=.8738   a=.8483

Curriculum Practice

34. Determines what changes took place as a result of the curriculum.
.2521   d   d

35. Provides information about the effectiveness of the curriculum.
.5642   .3484   .3264

36. Determines whether actions yielded predicted results.
.7197   .4447   .4984

37. Determines if objectives have been met.
.8437   .6849   .4540

38. Offers suggestions for curriculum modification.
.7489   .6115   .2716

39. Measures discrepancies between predetermined
objectives and outcomes.
.7268   .4538   .2727

40. Judges worth of instructional methods and materials.
.7419   .3860   .4624

41. Determines desired outcomes of instruction.
.7938   .4875   .6907

42. Improves curriculum programs.
.7506   .5714   .6040

Table 4.5 contd

ITEM-TOTAL CORRELATIONS

MWTCHR	SETCHR	PROFCURR
(N = 48)	(N = 37)	(N = 51)

VII. CURRICULUM EVALUATION

<u>Curriculum Practice</u>

43. Determines effectiveness of curriculum content.
.8234   .6981   .6923

44. Ascertains whether outcomes are the result of the curriculum.
.7085   .5979   .7627

45. Determines criteria to measure success of curriculum plan.
.7436   .8008   .6328

46. Identifies the strengths of curriculum content.
.7241   .7298   .5908

VIII. CURRICULUM POLICY
a=.7964   a=.6270   a=.7350

<u>Curriculum Practice</u>

47. Influences control of the curriculum.
.5965   .3817   b

48. Recommends what learning experience to include.
.6605   .2252   b

49. Mandates school goals.
.7015   .4958   .5309

50. States what ought to be taught.
.5781   .5127   .6497

51. Communicates with local and state government agencies.
.3763   c   .4942

Table 4.5 contd

ITEM-TOTAL CORRELATIONS

MWTCHR	SETCHR	PROFCURR
(N = 48)	(N = 37)	(N = 51)

IX. CURRICULUM AS A FIELD OF STUDY

a=.8697	a=.7786	a=.7092

Curriculum Practice

52. Promotes curriculum planning and implementation.

.7966	.6284	.2080

53. Organizes patterns and structures of curriculum.

.7637	.5774	.4157

54. Attempts to integrate theory and practice.

.6423	.5869	.6225

55. Analyzes structures of curriculum.

.6999	.5430	.4805

Notes: *a= The alpha correlation coefficient for each domain by Midwest and Southeast teachers and professors, that is, how the curriculum practices correlated within their respective domains.
b= Denotes that item was eliminated because it had an item total score of less than .20 according to the Professors of Curriculum ratings.
c = Denotes that item was eliminated because it had an item total score of less than .20 according to the Southeast teachers' ratings.
d = Denotes that item was eliminated because it had an item total score of less than .20 according to the Professors of Curriculum and Southeast teachers' ratings.

Ratings by the Midwest Teachers

Ratings for each of the subscales by the Midwest teacher sample demonstrated high levels of homogeneity All nine of the domains evidenced alpha coefficients of .70 or higher: curriculum evaluation (a=.93); curriculum design (a=.90; curriculum as a field of study (a=.

87); curriculum development (a=.87); curriculum research (a=.85); curriculum theory (a=.83); curriculum policy (a=.80); curriculum history (a=.78); and curriculum philosophy (a= .73)

Overall, forty-nine curriculum practices had alpha coefficients of .50 or higher and six had ranges of .20 to .49. (Refer to Table 4.6 and Figure 4.1, page 68, for graphic representation). The Midwest teachers evidenced considerable agreement in their ratings of the curriculum practices. Table 4.5 indicates that the Midwest teachers' tended to rate the curriculum practices higher than both the Southeast teachers and the Professors of Curriculum. Perhaps this is a reflection of the type of curriculum work they are engaged in, or an indication that they work with colleagues who share similar values concerning the importance of various curriculum practices.

Table 4.6
Number of Curriculum Practices within Designated Alpha Correlation Coefficient Ranges by Midwest Teachers (*MWTCHR*), Southeast Teachers (*SETCHR*), and the Professors of Curriculum (*PROFCURR*).

ALPHA CORRELATION COEFFICIENT RANGE

	.50 or HIGHER	.20 - .49	.20 or LOWER
SAMPLE GROUP			
MWTCHR N =48	49	6	
SETCHR N= 37	25	27	3
PROFCURR N= 51	28	21	6

Figure 4.1
Number of Curriculum Practices within Designated Alpha Correlation Coefficient Ranges by the Midwest Teachers (*MWTCHR*), Southeast Teachers (*SETCHR*), and the Professors of Curriculum (*PROFCURR*) for the Domains of   Curriculum

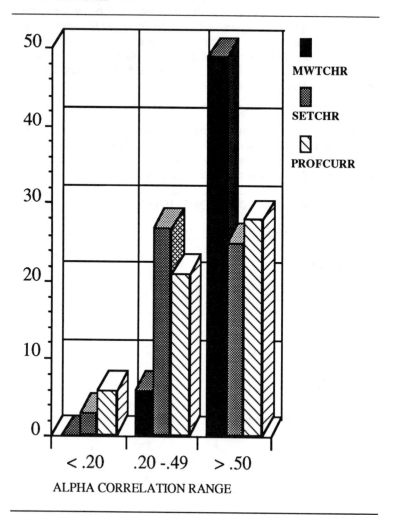

Ratings by the Southeast Teachers

High levels of homogeneity for the curriculum domains were demonstrated by the Southeast teacher group. Ratings by the Southeast teachers revealed that 6 of the curriculum domains had alpha coefficients of .70 or higher: curriculum evaluation (a=.87); curriculum design (a=.87); curriculum as a field of study (a=.78); curriculum development (a=.72); curriculum research (a=.70); and curriculum theory (a=.70). The remaining three domains had alpha correlations of .60 or higher: curriculum history (a=.65); curriculum philosophy (a=.64); and curriculum policy (a=.63). Once again, it should be noted that only 2 practices (mandates school goals and states what ought to be taught) remained in curriculum policy. This under representation represents a limitation of the instrument and the overall contribution of this domain should be considered somewhat questionable.

Ratings for the domains by Southeast teachers were found to be slightly lower than ratings by Midwest teachers and the Professors of Curriculum, although each of the subscales evidenced high levels of homogeneity. Curriculum practices with alpha correlation scores in the range of .50 or higher totaled 25. Twenty-seven (27) curriculum practices had alpha coefficients of .20 to .49. (Refer to Table 4.7). Once again it should be noted that three curriculum practices which had alpha correlation coefficients of less than .20 and were deleted from the instrument. Practices with insufficient alpha correlation scores were: determines the ends of education (domain: curriculum philosophy); determines what changes took place as a result of the curriculum (domain: curriculum evaluation); and communicates with local and state government agencies (domain: curriculum policy).   The Midwest teachers' ratings of the curriculum practices were slightly higher than those by the Southeast teachers. The differences in ratings between the Southeast and Midwest teachers might be a reflection of differences in teacher preparation training, pedagogical values, and institutional factors that influenced what teachers considered important practices.

Ratings by the Professors of Curriculum

Regarding ratings by the Professors of Curriculum, all of the curriculum domains, except curriculum development (a=.62) evidenced substantially high levels of homogeneity.   The remaining eight domains evidenced alpha coefficients of .70 or higher: curriculum design (a=.85); curriculum philosophy (a=.84); curriculum evaluation (a=.84); curriculum history (a=.76); curriculum research (a=.73); curriculum policy (a=.73); curriculum as a field of study (a=.71); and curriculum theory (a= .70).

Overall, excluding the six curriculum practices which had item discrimination scores of less than .20, twenty-eight curriculum practices had alpha coefficients of .50 or higher (See Table 4.7). Practices that were eliminated per the professors' ratings included three in the domain of curriculum development (develops curriculum guides, develops school grants, and addresses question of who will be involved in curriculum construction), one practice in curriculum evaluation (determines what changes took place as a result of the curriculum), and two practices in curriculum policy (influences control of the curriculum and recommends what learning experiences to include). An overview of the ratings of curriculum practices by the Professors of Curriculum and the Southeast teachers demonstrated that there was a comparable number of items in the ranges of .50 and higher, (28 and 25 respectively) and .20 to .49, (21 and 27 respectively). The fact that the Professors of Curriculum are not engaged in curriculum work on an everyday basis or work with colleagues who participate in similar roles and behaviors might account for the ratings they assigned to the curriculum practices.

Figure 4.2
Midwest Teachers (*MWTCHR*), Southeast Teachers (*SETCHR*), and the Professors of Curriculum (*PROFCURR*) Ratings of the Domains of Curriculum by Alpha Correlations.

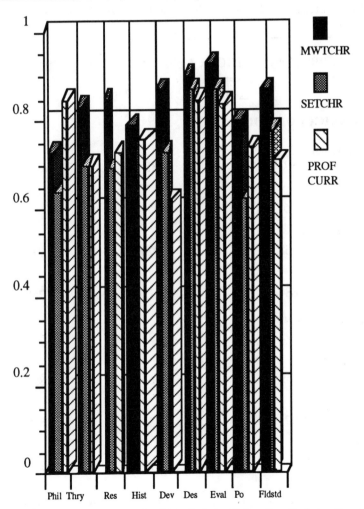

Legend: Phil = Curriculum Philosophy; Thry= Curriculum Theory; Res= Curriculum Research; Hist = Curriculum History; Dev = Curriculum Development; Des = Curriculum Design; Eval = Curriculum Evaluation; Po = Curriculum Policy; Fldstd = Curriculum as a Field of Study

Table 4.7
The Importance of Curriculum Domains as Indicated by Alpha Correlation Coefficient Scores by the Midwest Teachers (*MWTCHR*), Southeast Teachers (*SETCHR*), and the Professors of Curriculum (*PROFCURR*) in Order of Rank.

MWTCHR Alpha* (N =48) Rank		SETCHR Alpha (N = 37) Rank		PROFCURR Alpha (N =51) Rank	
CURRICULUM DOMAIN					
PHILOSOPHY					
9	.7307	8	.6435	3	.8450
THEORY					
6	.8306	5	.6950	8	.6974
RESEARCH					
5	.8468	6	.6920	6	.7340
HISTORY					
8	.7884	7	.6473	4	.7580
DEVELOPMENT					
4	.8695	4	.7278	9	.6236
DESIGN					
2	.9049	2	.8663	1	.8505
EVALUATION					
1	.9332	1	.8738	2	.8483
POLICY					
7	.7964	9	.6270	5	.7350
FIELD OF STUDY					
3	.8697	3	.7786	7	.7092

Note: Alpha* = Denotes alpha correlation coefficient score

Rank Order Importance of the Curriculum Domains

Table 4.7 shows that the Midwest and Southeast teachers ranked curriculum evaluation, curriculum design, curriculum as a field of study and curriculum development in ranks 1 through 4 respectively. The Midwest teachers rated curriculum research and curriculum theory in ranks 5 and 6; the Southeast teachers rated the same domains in ranks 6 and 5. Midwest teachers ranked curriculum policy, curriculum history and curriculum philosophy in ranks 7, 8, and 9 respectively. The Southeast teachers rated these three domains in ranks 9, 7, and 8 respectively. Figure 2 (see page 71) presents the same data in graphic form.

The Professors of Curriculum ranked curriculum design and curriculum evaluation as 1 and 2. The Midwest and Southeast teacher groups rated the respective domains as 2 and 1. Only one other similarity was noted between the Professors of Curriculum and the Midwest and Southeast teacher groups rank order ratings of the domains. The professors rated curriculum research as rank order 6, concurring with the Southeast teachers; the Midwest teachers rated this domain as rank order 5.

Regarding the importance of curriculum domains in order of rank, the results shown in Table 4.7 demonstrate that the Midwest and Southeast teacher groups tended to rate the curriculum domains more similarly than the Professors of Curriculum. These findings might be a reflection that teachers work with colleagues who are involved in similar kinds of activities, roles and behaviors on an everyday basis. Irrespective of the ranking of domains by the Midwest and Southeast teachers and Professors of Curriculum, it is notable that every domain evidenced a high level of homogeneity, with alphas ranging from .62 to .93.

The nine domains represent the broad areas of knowledge important to the field of curriculum and suggest what curriculum specialists should know about the field. The 47 curriculum practices categorized within the domains represent important activities that describe what curriculum specialists do. Together the curriculum domains and curriculum practices represent the knowledge base of the field and a partial compendium of behaviors that curriculum specialists engage in while inquiring about planning and implementing the curriculum.

Table 4.8
Item-total Correlations and Alpha Coefficients for the Importance and Coverage of Curriculum Practices within the Domains of Curriculum by the Professors of Curriculum

DOMAINS OF CURRICULUM

I. CURRICULUM PHILOSOPHY

Item-total   Item-total
Correlation   Correlation

Importance   Coverage

Curriculum Practice

1. Reflecting upon schools of thought including:
perennialism; essentialism; progressivism; reconstructionism;
and existentialism.
.7025   .2923

2. Determines the ends of education
.4880   .5602

3.Determines an orientation to curriculum.
.6799   .3149

4. Suggests a view of society and students in relationship to education.
.5323   .5070

5. States the purpose of education.
.6428   .5420

6. Elaborates on the theory of curriculum.
.7101   .4952

Alpha coefficient = .8450 Alpha coefficient = .7294

Table 4.8 contd

II. CURRICULUM THEORY

Item-total Correlation	Item-total Correlation
Importance	Coverage

Curriculum Practice

7. Creates statements that give meaning to a school curriculum.

.6467	.6159

8. Uses techniques of science and logic to present a systematic view of phenomena.

.4298	.5007

9. Deals with structuring knowledge.

.4969	.4748

10. Identifies how students learn.

.4237	.4957

11. Uses principles and rules to study curriculum.

.2630	.2235

Alpha coefficient = .6974   Alpha coefficient = .7036

Table 4.8 contd

III. CURRICULUM RESEARCH

Item-total   Item-total
Correlation   Correlation

Importance   Coverage

Curriculum Practice

12. Analyzes resisting and supporting forces.
.4059   .4163

13. Advances hypotheses and assumptions of the field.
.5783   .4728

14. Uses systematic inquiry for the purpose of solving a particular problem.
.4473   .2463

15. Analyzes steps to be taken in problem solving.
5201   .2968

16. Focuses on research and/or inquiry of curriculum.
.5243   .4542

Alpha coefficient = .7340   Alpha coefficient = .6303

Table 4.8 contd

IV. CURRICULUM HISTORY

Item-total Correlation	Item-total Correlation
Importance	Coverage

Curriculum Practice
17. Describes past curriculum thought and practices.

.4127	.5049

18. Interprets past curriculum practice.

.7323	.8000

19. Provides a chronology of important events in curriculum.

.5725	.4349

20. Examines forces that inhibit curriculum innovations.

.2322	*

Alpha coeffiecient = .7580 Alpha coefficient = .7722

Table 4.8 contd

V. CURRICULUM DEVELOPMENT

Item-total Correlation	Item-total Correlation
Importance	Coverage

Curriculum Practice

21. Develops curriculum guides.
*   *

22. Develops school grants.
*   *

23. Determines procedures necessary for curriculum plan.
.1988   .2398

24. Addresses question of who will be involved in curriculum construction.
*   .4242

25. Integrates content and learning experiences.
.4917   .5509

26. Decides on nature and organization of curriculum.
.6499   .5064

Alpha coefficient = .6236   Alpha coefficient = .6413

contd

URRICULUM POLICY

Item-total
Correlation

Coverage

Practice

es the control of the curriculum.
*

ends what learning experiences to include.
.2214

s school goals.
.5109

hat ought to be taught.
.5782

cates with local and state governments agencies.
.3209

nt = .7350   Alpha coefficient = .6394

Table 4.8 contd

VI. CURRICULUM DESIGN

Item-total Correlation	Item-total Correlation
Importance	Coverage

Curriculum Practice

27. Attempts to define what subject matter took place as a result of the curriculum.
.6288   .6552

28. Guides program development for individual students.
.7463   .7764

29. Selects subject matter and learning experiences.
.6173   .6359

30. Establishes the primary focus of subject matter.
.7389   .5562

31. Permits curriculum ideas to function.
.4871   .4839

32. Integrates careful planning.
.7631   .7608

33. Indicates instructional strategies to be utilized.
.3492   .2068

Alpha coefficients = .8505 Alpha coefficient = .8257

Table 4.8 contd

VII. CURRICULUM EVALUATION

Item-total Correlation	Item-total Correlation
Importance	Coverage

Curriculum Practice

34. Determines what changes took place as a result of the curriculum.
*   .3360

35. Provides information about the effectiveness of the curriculum.
.3264   .5392

36. Determines wheter actions yielded predicted results.
.4984   .4839

37. Determines if objectives have been met.
.4540   .3659

38. Offers suggestions for curriculum modification.
.2716   .5154

39. Measures discrepancies between predetermined objectives and outcomes.
.2727   .3211

40. Judges worth of instructional methods and materials.
.4624   .3834

41. Determines desired outcomes of instruction.
.6907   .5576

42. Improves curriculum programs.
.6040   .4501

Table 4.8 contd

VII. CURRICULUM EVALUATI

Item-total Correlation	Item-total Correlation
Importance	Coverage

Curriculum Practice

43. Determines effectiveness of curr
.6923   .6704

44. Ascertains whether outcomes a
.7697   .7604

45. Determines criteria to measur
.6328   .5721

46. Identifies the strengths of cu
.5908   .425

Alpha coefficient = .8483   Alp

Table 4.

VIII.

Item-total Correlatio

Importanc

Curriculum

47. Influen
*

48. Recomm
*

49. Mandate
.5309

50. States w
.6497

51. Communi
.4942

Alpha coeffici

Table 4.8 contd

IX. CURRICULUM AS A FIELD OF STUDY

Item-total Correlation	Item-total Correlation
Importance	Coverage

Curriculum Practice

52. Promotes curriculum planning and implementation.
.2080   *

53. Organizes patterns and structures of curriculum.
.4157   .4657

54. Attempts to integrate theory and practice.
.6225   .3939

55. Analyzes structures of curriculum.
.4805   .3151

Alpha coefficient = .7092   Alpha coefficient = .6134

* = Denotes alpha correlation coefficient was lower than .20 and item was eliminated.

Results Related to Research Question 5

Importance and Coverage of Curriculum Practices within the Domains of Curriculum by the Professors of Curriculum

Ratings of Importance

Table 4.8 shows the alpha coefficients for each subscale and the related curriculum practices within the domains of curriculum. As previously described, based on the low end item inclusion cut off score of .20, the following curriculum practices (items) were eliminated: curriculum evaluation (determines what changes took place as a result of the curriculum); curriculum policy (influences control of the curriculum; and recommends what learning experiences to include); and curriculum development (develops curriculum guides, develops school grants, and addresses question of who will be involved in curriculum construction). After these items were eliminated, the alpha correlation coefficients were recomputed. The discussion of the results that follow reflects these recalculations.

Regarding the rankings of the importance of curriculum practices, four subscales within the domains of curriculum evidenced high alpha coefficients (greater than + or -.75): curriculum philosophy (a = .85); curriculum design (a = .85); curriculum evaluation (a = .84); and curriculum history (a = .76). Five subscales revealed mid range alpha (+ or -.50 to .75) coefficients including: curriculum policy (a = .74); curriculum research (a = .73); curriculum as a field of study (a = . 71); curriculum theory (a = .70); and curriculum development (a = . 62).

Ratings of Coverage

Table 4.8 shows the alpha coefficients for the coverage of curriculum practices within domains of curriculum. Two curriculum practices (items) did not meet the low end inclusion cut off score criterion. Those items that were eliminated include: curriculum history (examines forces that inhibit history); and curriculum as a field of study (promotes curriculum planning and implementation); as well as items that were also eliminated in the ratings for the importance of curriculum practices with the domains of curriculum, including: curriculum policy (influences control of the curriculum); and curriculum development (develops curriculum guides and develops school guides).

Once again, alpha correlations were recalculated. The corrected reliability assessment showed that, regarding the ratings of coverage for curriculum practices within the domains of curriculum, three subscales evidenced high range alpha coefficients (greater than + or - .75) including: curriculum evaluation (a = . 84); curriculum design (a = .83); and curriculum history (a = .77). Alpha coefficients in the mid range (+ or -. 50 to . 75) were six subscales: curriculum philosophy (a = .73); curriculum theory (a = .70); curriculum policy (a = .64); curriculum development (a = .64); curriculum research (a = .63); and curriculum as a field of study (a = . 61).

The professors' ratings, showed that two domains (curriculum evaluation and curriculum design) demonstrated a high level of homogeneity for both the importance and coverage of curriculum practices. Perhaps the concrete and definitive nature of the curriculum practices in these two subscales was the reason for their high levels of internal consistency. Curriculum history demonstrated internal consistency that was at the upper end of the mid range and at the lower end of the high range for ratings of importance and coverage. Curriculum theory, curriculum research, curriculum development, curriculum policy, and curriculum as a field of study demonstrated a mid-high level of internal consistency for both importance and coverage of curriculum practices. Curriculum philosophy showed a high range of internal consistency for the importance and mid range level of internal consistency for coverage of curriculum practices. The findings related to curriculum philosophy suggest that the items in this subscale demonstrated greater homogeneity when ranked for importance than when rated for the extent of coverage they received in textbooks selected by Professors of Curriculum.

Curriculum Practices and Domains of Curriculum: Final Version

Table 4.9 shows the final version for curriculum practices within the domains of curriculum excluding items that had Cronbach alpha correlations of less than .20 per the teachers' and professors' ratings. Taken as a whole, the homogeneity as evidenced by ratings of importance for the domain subscales evidenced alpha coefficients ranging from .62 to .85. Table 4.9 shows only the domains and statements which describe the related curriculum practices as per ratings of importance. Curriculum practices that were deleted as a result of having an alpha correlation coefficient of .20 or lower are designated by an asterisk (*).

With respect to ratings of importance, forty-seven of the fifty-five curriculum practices within nine domains of curriculum were retained. It should be noted that in the final instrument, curriculum development had only three items and curriculum policy had only two items. This should be considered a limiting feature of the instrument. This instrument also reflects the elimination of two domains (curriculum change and curriculum implementation). These subscales were deleted as the result of the independent categorization process by the expert judges.

Table 4.9
The Domains of Curriculum and Related Curriculum Practices as per the Ratings of the Midwest Teachers (*MWTCHR*), Southeast Teachers (*SETCHR*), and the Professors of Curriculum (*PROFCURR*): FINAL VERSION

DOMAINS OF CURRICULUM

I. CURRICULUM PHILOSOPHY

Curriculum Practice

1. Reflecting upon schools of thought including: perennialism; essentialism; progressivism; reconstructionism; and existentialism.

2. Determines the ends of education. *

3. Determines an orientation to curriculum.

4. Suggests a view of society and students in relationship to education.

5. States the purposes of education.

6. Elaborates on the theory of curriculum.

II. CURRICULUM THEORY

Curriculum Practice

7. Creates statements that give meaning to a school curriculum.

8. Uses techniques of science and logic to present a systematic view of phenomena.

9. Deals with structuring knowledge.

10. Identifies how students learn.

11. Uses principles and rules to study curriculum.

Table 4.9 contd

III. CURRICULUM RESEARCH

Curriculum Practice

12. Analyzes resisting and supporting forces.

13. Advances hypotheses and assumptions of the field.

14. Uses systematic inquiry for the purpose of solving a particular problem.

15. Analyzes steps to be taken in problem solving.

16. Focuses on research and/or inquiry of curriculum.

IV. CURRICULUM HISTORY

Curriculum Practice

17. Describes past curriculum thought and practices.

18. Interprets past curriculum practice.

19. Provides a chronology of important event in curriculum.

20. Examines forces that inhibit curriculum innovations.

Table 4.9 contd

V. CURRICULUM DEVELOPMENT

Curriculum Practice

21. Develops curriculum guides. *

22. Develops school grants. *

23. Determines procedures necessary for a curriculum plan.

24. Addresses question of who will be involved in curriculum construction. *

25. Integrates content and learning experiences.

26. Decides on nature and organization of curriculum.

VI. CURRICULUM DESIGN

Curriculum Practice

27. Attempts to define what subject matter will be used.

28. Guides program development for individual students.

29. Selects subject matter and learning experiences.

30. Establishes the primary focus of subject matter.

31. Permits curriculum ideas to function.

32. Integrates careful planning.

33. Indicates instructional strategies to be utilized.

Table 4.9 contd

VII. CURRICULUM EVALUATION

<u>Curriculum Practice</u>

34. Determines what changes took place as a result of the curriculum.*

35. Provides information about the effectiveness of the curriculum.

36. Determines whether actions yielded predicted results.

37. Determines if objectives have been met.

38. Offers suggestions for curriculum modification.

39. Measures discrepancies between predetermined objectives and outcomes.

40. Judges worth of instructional methods and materials.

41. Determines desired outcomes of instruction.

42. Improves curriculum programs.

43. Determines effectiveness of curriculum content.

44. Ascertains whether outcomes are the result of the curriculum.

45. Determines criteria to measure success of curriculum plan.

46. Identifies the strengths of curriculum content.

Table 4.9 contd

VIII. CURRICULUM POLICY

<u>Curriculum Practice</u>

47. Influences control of the curriculum. *

48. Recommends what learning experiences to include. *

49. Mandates school goals.

50. States what ought to be taught.

51. Communicates with local and state government.*

IX. CURRICULUM AS A FIELD OF STUDY

<u>Curriculum Practice</u>

52. Promotes curriculum planning and implementation.

53. Organizes patterns and structures of curriculum.

54. Attempts to integrate theory and practice.

55. Analyzes structures of curriculum.

* = Denotes that item was deleted as a result of an alpha correlation score of .20 or lower per the teachers' and/or professors' ratings.

Importance of Curriculum Practices per Mean Scores

Mean scores in the range of 1-2, denoted that items were very unimportant. Ranges of 2-3, denoted that items were fairly unimportant, scores in the range of 3-4 indicated that items were of some importance, and items with mean scores greater than 4 demonstrated that items were fairly important, as per the Likert scale. In terms of importance, eight mean curriculum practices were ranked as fairly unimportant; thirty-two were ranked as being of some importance; and fifteen were ranked as fairly important. Tables 4.10, 4.11 and 4.12 show the rank ordered mean response for the importance of each curriculum practice by the Midwest and Southeast teachers and the Professors of Curriculum respectively. Table 4.14 shows the total mean for each domain subscale according to the teachers' and professors' ratings.

Table 4.10
Mean Responses for the Importance of the Domains of Curriculum by the Midwest Teachers (N = 48) in Order of Rank.

<u>Curriculum Domain</u>	<u>Importance</u>	<u>Rank</u>

<u>Curriculum Practice</u>
1. Integrates content and learning experiences.

| (CD) | 4.1875 | 1 |

2. Guides program development for individual students.

| (DE) | 4.1250 | 2.5 |

3. Indicates instructional strategies to be utilized.

| (DE) | 4.1250 | 2.5 |

4. Identifies the strengths of curriculum content.

| (CE) | 4.0625 | 4 |

5. Integrates careful planning.

| (DE) | 3.9792 | 5 |

6. Offers suggestions for curriculum modification.

| (CE) | 3.9583 | 8 |

Table 4.10 contd

Curriculum Domain	Importance	Rank

Curriculum Practice

7. Promotes curriculum planning and implementation.

(CF)	3.9583	8

8. Improves curriculum programs.

(CE)	3.9583	8

9. Identifies how students learn.

(CT)	3.9583	8

10. Analyzes steps to be taken in problem solving.

(CR)	3.9583	8

11. Determines if objectives have been met.

(CE)	3.9375	11.5

12. Determines desired outcomes of instruction.

(CE)	3.9375	11.5

13. Permits curriculum ideas to function.

(DE)	3.9167	13

14. Establishes the primary focus of subject matter.

(DE)	3.8750	14.5

15. Selects subject matter and learning experiences.

(DE)	3.8750	14.5

16. Determines criteria to measure success of curriculum plan.

(CE)	3.8333	16

17. Determines effectiveness of curriculum content.

(CE)	3.7917	18

18. Determines whether actions yielded predicted results.

(CE)	3.7917	18

Table 4.10 contd

Curriculum Domain	Importance	Rank

Curriculum Practice

19. Judges worth of instructional methods and materials.
(CE)   3.7917   18

20. Uses techniques of science and logic to present a systematic view of phenomena.
(CT)   3.7708   18

21. Deals with structuring knowledge.
(CT)   3.7500   24

22. Suggests a view of society and students in relationship to education.
(CP)   3.7500   24

23. Examines forces that inhibit curriculum innovations.
(CH)   3.7500   24

24. Creates statements that give meaning to a school curriculum.
(CT)   3.7500   24

25. Attempts to define what subject matter will be used.
(DE)   3.7500   24

26. Uses systematic inquiry for the purpose of solving a particular problem.
(CR)   3.7500   24

27. Ascertains whether outcomes are the result of the curriculum.
(CE)   3.7500   24

28. Develops curriculum guides.
(CD)   3.7500   24

29. Provides information about the effectiveness of the curriculum.
(CE)   3.7451   29

Table 4.10 contd

Curriculum Domain	Importance	Rank

Curriculum Practice

30. Attempts to integrate theory and practice.
(CF)   3.6875   30

31. Organizes patterns and structures of curriculum.
(CF)   3.6667   31

32. Decides on nature and organization of curriculum.
(CD)   3.7292   32

33. Focuses on research and/or inquiry of curriculum.
(CR)   3.7083   33

34. States what ought to be taught.
(PO)   3.6250   34.5

35. Determines procedures necessary for a curriculum plan.
(CD)   3.6250   34.5

36. Provides a chronology of important event in curriculum.
(CH)   3.6042   36

37. Determines an orientation to curriculum.
(CP)   3.5625   37

38. States the purposes of education.
(CP)   3.5417   38

39. Analyzes structures of curriculum.
(CF)   3.5208   39

40. Measures discrepancies between predetermined objectives and outcomes.
(CE)   3.4792   40

Table 4.10 contd

Curriculum Domain	Importance	Rank

Curriculum Practice

41. Advances hypotheses and assumptions of the field.
(CR)   3.4375   41

42. Determines what changes took place as a result of the curriculum.
(CE)   3.4167   42.5

43. Develops school guides.
(CD)   3.4167   42.5

44. Recommends what learning experiences to include.
(PO)   3.4000   44

45. Uses principles and rules to study curriculum.
(CT)   3.3342   45

46. Interprets past curriculum practice.
(CH)   3.3125   46

47. Mandates school goals.
(PO)   3.2917   47

48. Addresses question of who will be involved in curriculum construction.
(CD)   3.2708   48

49. Analyzes resisting and supporting forces.
(CR)   3.2500   50

50. Communicates with local and state government agencies.
(PO)   3.2500   50

Table 4.10 contd

<u>Curriculum Domain</u>   <u>Importance</u>   <u>Rank</u>

<u>Curriculum Practice</u>

51. Influences the control of the curriculum.
(PO)   3.2500   50

52. Determines the ends of education.
(CP)   3.2292   52

53. Elaborates on the theory of curriculum.
(CP)   3.1875   53

54. Describes past curriculum thought and practices.
(CH)   3.1250   54

55. Reflecting upon schools of thought including: perennialism; essentialism; progressivism; reconstructionism; and existentialism.
(CP)   2.3750   55

Notes: <u>Importance</u>
                              5 = very important
                              4 = fairly important
                              3 = some importance
                              2 = fairly unimportant
                              1 = very unimportant

<u>DOMAINS OF CURRICULUM:</u> CP = curriculum philosophy, CT = curriculum theory, CR = curriculum research, CH = curriculum history, CD = curriculum development, DE= curriculum design, CE= curriculum evaluation, PO = curriculum policy, CF = curriculum as a field of study

Rankings of Domain Practices by the Midwest Teachers

Table 4.10 shows the mean responses of the domains of curriculum and related practices in order of rank by the Midwest teachers. One curriculum practice was rated as fairly unimportant (curriculum practices #55), fifty curriculum practices were rated of some importance (curriculum practices #5 - #54), and four were rated as fairly important (curriculum practices #1 - #4). Mean responses ranged from 4.18 to 2.38. Curriculum practices in the domains of curriculum development, curriculum design, curriculum design, curriculum evaluation, curriculum design were assigned to the first five respective ranks. Five practices that tied for rank eight were in the following domains: curriculum evaluation; curriculum as a field of study; curriculum evaluation; curriculum theory; and curriculum research. The last seven consecutive ranks (49 - 55) were held by three curriculum practices within the domain of curriculum philosophy, 2 practices in curriculum policy, and one practice in curriculum history and curriculum research. It should be noted that two practices in curriculum policy and one practice in curriculum research tied for rank order 50.

In contrast to the Professors of Curriculum, the Midwest teachers rated the first five ranked practices in domains of curriculum development, curriculum design and curriculum evaluation. These domains generally evidenced greater agreement regarding ratings of importance per the teacher rankings. (The professors rated 2 curriculum practices in curriculum philosophy, and one practice in curriculum design, curriculum history and curriculum as a field of study in the first five consecutive ranks). The teachers' data indicates less agreement on the ratings of importance for practices in curriculum philosophy and curriculum policy. The lack of agreement regarding the rating of importance for practices in curriculum policy is consistent with the disagreement demonstrated by the Professors of Curriculum.

Table 4.11
Mean Responses for the Importance of the Domains of Curriculum by the Southeast Teachers (N = 37) in Order of Rank.

Curriculum Domain   Importance   Rank

Curriculum Practice

1. Provides information about the effectiveness of the curriculum.
(CE)   4.0811   1

2. Determines if objectives have been met.
(CE)   4.0541   2

3. Integrates careful planning.
(DE)   4.0270   3

4. Develops curriculum guides.
(CD)   4.0000   4.5

5. Guides program development for individual students.
(DE)   4.0000   4.5

6. Establishes the primary focus of subject matter.
(DE)   3.9730   6

7. Recommends what learning experiences to include.
(PO)   3.8649   8

8. Attempts to define what subject matter will be used.
(DE)   3.8649   8

9. Permits curriculum ideas to function.
(DE)   3.8649   8

10. Determines whether actions yielded predicted results.
(CE)   3.8919   10

Table 4.11 contd

Curriculum Domain	Importance	Rank

Curriculum Practice

11. Integrates content and learning experiences.
(CD)   3.8378   12

12. Offers suggestions for curriculum modification.
(CE)   3.8378   12

13. Uses systematic inquiry for the purpose of solving a particular problem.
(CR)   3.8378   12

14. Analyzes steps to be taken in problem solving.
(CR)   3.7838   14

15. Selects subject matter and learning experiences.
(DE)   3.8108   15.5

16. Identifies the strengths of curriculum content.
(CE)   3.8108   15.5

17. Determines desired outcomes of instruction.
(CE)   3.7568   17.5

18. Promotes curriculum planning and implementation.
(CF)   3.7568   17.5

19. Creates statements that give meaning to a school curriculum.
(CT)   3.7027   19.5

20. Indicates instructional strategies to be utilized.
(DE)   3.7027   19.5

Table 4.11 contd

Curriculum Domain	Importance	Rank

Curriculum Practice

21. Determines an orientation to curriculum.
(CP)   3.6757   23

22. Determines what changes took place as a result of the curriculum.
(CE)   3.6757   23

23. Organizes patterns and structures of curriculum.
(CF)   3.6757   23

24. Deals with structuring knowledge.
(CT)   3.6757   23

25. Determines procedures necessary for a curriculum plan.
(CD)   3.6486   25

26. Improves curriculum programs.
(CE)   3.6216   26

27. Identifies how students learn.
(CT)   3.5946   27.5

28. Attempts to integrate theory and practice.
(CF)   3.5946   27.5

29. Develops school grants.
(CD)   3.5676   29.5

30. States what ought to be taught.
(PO)   3.5676   29.5

Table 4.11 contd

Curriculum Domain	Importance	Rank

Curriculum Practice

31. Provides a chronology of important events in curriculum.
(CH)   3.5405   31

32. Determines effectiveness of curriculum content.
(CE)   3.5135   34

33. Determines criteria to measure success of curriculum plan.
(CE)   3.5135   34

34. Influences control of the curriculum.
(PO)   3.5135   34

35. Suggests a view of society and students in relationship to education.
(CP)   3.5135   34

36. States the purposes of education.
(CP)   3.4324   37

37. Uses principles and rules to study curriculum.
(CT)   3.4324   37

38. Judges worth of instructional methods and materials.
(CE)   3.4324   37

39. Describes past curriculum thought and practices.
(CH)   3.3784   39

40. Uses techniques of science and logic to present a systematic view of phenomena.
(CT)   3.3243   42

Table 4.11 contd

Curriculum Domain	Importance	Rank

Curriculum Practice

41. Addresses question of who will be involved in curriculum construction.
(CD)   3.3243   42

42. Ascertains whether outcomes are the result of the curriculum.
(CE)   3.3243   42

43. Decides on nature and organization of curriculum.
(CD)   3.2973   42

44. Determines the ends of education.
(CP)   3.2973   44.5

45. Measures discrepancies between predetermined objectives and outcomes.
(CE)   3.2973   44.5

46. Elaborates on the theory of curriculum.
(CP)   3.2703   46

47. Focuses on research and/or inquiry of curriculum.
(CR)   3.2432   47

48. Examines forces that inhibit curriculum innovations.
(CH)   3.2162   50

49. Communicates with local and state government.
(PO)   3.2162   50

50. Analyzes structures of curriculum.
(CF)   3.2162   50

Table 4.11 contd

Curriculum Domain	Importance	Rank

Curriculum Practice

51. Mandates school goals.
(PO)   3.1892   51

52. Reflecting upon schools of thought including: perennialism; essentialism; progressivism; reconstructionism; and existentialism.

(CP)   3.1622   52.5

53. Analyzes resisting and supporting forces.
(CR)   3.1622   52.5

54. Interprets past curriculum practice.
(CH)   3.1351   54

55. Advances hypotheses and assumptions of the field.
(CR)   3.0541   55

Notes: Importance
                              5 = very important
                              4 = fairly important
                              3 = some importance
                              2 = fairly unimportant
                              1 = very unimportant

DOMAINS OF CURRICULUM: CP = curriculum philosophy, CT = curriculum theory, CR = curriculum research, CH = curriculum history, CD = curriculum development, DE= curriculum design, CE= curriculum evaluation, PO = curriculum policy, CF = curriculum as a field of study

Rankings of Domain Practices by the Southeast Teachers

Table 4.11 shows the mean responses of the domains of curriculum and related practices in order of rank by the Southeast teachers. Mean responses ranged from 4.08 to 3.05. Five curriculum practices were rated as fairly important (curriculum practices #1 - #5); fifty practices were rated as of some importance (curriculum practices #6 - #55). These findings are comparable to the ratings assigned by the Midwest teachers. As previously discussed, the Midwest teachers rated four practices as fairly important, 50 practices as of some importance, and one practice as fairly unimportant. The Southeast teachers rated three curriculum practices in the domains of curriculum design, two practices in curriculum evaluation, and one practice in both curriculum development and curriculum policy occupied the first seven ranks. Of the last seven ranks (49-55), there were two practices in curriculum policy and curriculum research, and one in the domains of curriculum as a field of study, curriculum philosophy, and curriculum history.

A comparison of the Midwest and Southeast teachers revealed that the Southeast teachers assigned practices in the domains of curriculum evaluation and curriculum development to the first five ranks as did the Midwest teachers. Per the Southeast teacher ratings, there was greater agreement as to the importance of these domains. An overview of the responses by the Professors of Curriculum, Midwest, and Southeast teachers indicated that there was less agreement by all the respondent groups in their ratings of importance for practices in curriculum philosophy and curriculum policy.

TABLE 4.12
Mean Responses for the Importance of Domains of Curriculum by the Professors of Curriculum (N = 51) in Order of Rank.

Domains of Curriculum	Importance	Rank

Curriculum Practice

1. Suggests a view of society and students in relationship to education.
(CP)   4.3922   1

2. Determines an orientation to curriculum.
(CP)   4.3529   2.5

Table 4.12 contd
Domains of Curriculum   Importance   Rank

Curriculum Practice

3. Permits curriculum ideas to function.
(DE)   4.3529   2.5

4. Attempts to integrate theory and practice.
(CF)   4.3137   4

5. Describes past curriculum thought and practices.
(CH)   4.2745   5

6. Focuses on research and/or inquiry of curriculum.
(CR)   4.2157   6

7. Elaborates on the theory of curriculum.
(CP)   4.1961   7

8. Advances hypotheses and assumptions of the field.
(CR)   4.1765   8.5

9. Organizes patterns and structures of curriculum.
(CF)   4.1765   8.5

10. Deals with structuring knowledge.
(CT)   4.1569   10

11. States the purposes of education.
(CP)   4.1176   11

12. Determines what changes took place as a result of the curriculum.
(CE)   4.0980   12

13. Reflecting upon schools of thought including: perennialism; essentialism; progressivism; reconstructionism; and existentialism.
(CP)   4.0588   13

14. Analyzes structures of curriculum.
(CF)   4.0392   14

Table 4.12 contd

Domains of Curriculum	Importance	Rank

Curriculum Practice

15. Examines forces that inhibit curriculum innovations.

(CH)	4.0196	15

16. Addresses question of who will be involved in curriculum construction.

(CD)	3.9804	16

17. Integrates content and learning experiences.

(CD)	3.9608	18

18. Creates statements that give meaning to a school curriculum.

(CT)	3.9608	18

19. Influences the control of the curriculum.

(PO)	3.9608	18

20. Determines the ends of education.

(CP)	3.9412	20

21. Decides on nature and organization of curriculum.

(CD)	3.8824	21

22. Interprets past curriculum practice.

(CH)	3.8627	22

23. Offers suggestions for curriculum modification.

(CE)	3.7647	23

24. Uses principles and rules to study curriculum.

(CT)	3.7843	24

25. Provides information about the effectiveness of the curriculum.

(CE)	3.7451	26

26. Identifies the strengths of curriculum content.

(CE)	3.7451	26

Table 4.12 contd

Domains of Curriculum	Importance	Rank

Curriculum Practice

27. Analyzes resisting and supporting forces.
(CR)   3.7451   26

28. Establishes the primary focus of subject matter.
(DE)   3.7059   28.5

29. Provides a chronology of important event in curriculum.
(CH)   3.7059   28.5

30. Promotes curriculum planning and implementation.
(CF)   3.6863   30

31. Integrates careful planning.
(DE)   3.6853   31

32. Selects subject matter and learning experiences.
(DE)   3.6667   32.5

33. Determines criteria to measure success of curriculum plan.
(CE)   3.6667   32.5

34. Attempts to define what subject matter will be used.
(DE)   3.5882   34

35. Improves curriculum programs.
(CE)   3.5098   35

36. Determines if objectives have been met.
(CE)   3.4706   36

37. Determines procedures necessary for a curriculum plan.
(CD)   3.4510   37

Table 4.12 contd

Domains of Curriculum	Importance	Rank

Curriculum Practice

38. Uses techniques of science and logic to present a systematic view of phenomena.

(CT)	3.4313	38

39. Guides program development for individual students.

(DE)	3.4118	39

40. Identifies how students learn.

(CT)	3.4092	40

41. Determines effectiveness of curriculum content.

(CE)	3.3922	41

42. Analyzes steps to be taken in problem solving.

(CR)	3.2941	42

43. Determines whether actions yielded predicted results.

(CE)	3.2745	43

44. Uses systematic inquiry for the purpose of solving a particular problem.

(CR)	3.2157	44

45. Judges worth of instructional methods and materials.

(CE)	3.1765	45.5

46. Ascertains whether outcomes are the result of the curriculum.

(CE)	3.1765	45.5

47. Recommends what learning experiences to include.

(PO)	3.0196	47

48. Determines desired outcomes of instruction.

(CE)	2.9412	48

Table 4.12 contd

Domains of Curriculum	Importance	Rank

Curriculum Practice

49. Indicates instructional strategies to be utilized.
(DE)   2.7843   49

50. States what ought to be taught.
(PO)   2.7647   50

51. Communicates with local and state government agencies.
(PO)   2.5882   51

52. Mandates school goals.
(PO)   2.4706   52

53. Measures discrepancies between predetermined objectives and outcomes.
(CE)   2.4510   53.5

54. Develops curriculum guides.
(CD)   2.4510   53.5

55. Develops school grants.
(CD)   2.0784   55

Notes: Importance
                        5 = very important
                        4 = fairly important
                        3 = some importance
                        2 = fairly unimportant
                        1 = very unimportant

DOMAINS OF CURRICULUM: CP = curriculum philosophy, CT = curriculum theory, CR = curriculum research, CH = curriculum history, CD = curriculum development, DE= curriculum design, CE= curriculum evaluation, PO = curriculum policy, CF = curriculum as a field of study

Rankings of Domain Practices by the Professors of Curriculum

Table 4.12 shows the mean responses of the domains of curriculum and related practices in order of rank by the Professors of Curriculum. Eight curriculum practices were rated as fairly unimportant (curriculum practices #48 - #55), thirty-two were rated of some importance (curriculum practices #16 - #47), and fifteen were rated as fairly important (curriculum practices #1 - #15). Mean responses range from 4.39 to 2.08.

Curriculum practices in the curriculum philosophy, curriculum philosophy, curriculum design, curriculum as a field of study, curriculum history, curriculum research and curriculum philosophy domains were ranked 1, 2.5, 2.5, 4, 5, 6, and 7 respectively. Curriculum practices in the more traditional domains: curriculum philosophy; curriculum research; curriculum history; and curriculum as a field of study were ranked higher than curriculum practices in the domains of curriculum evaluation, curriculum design, and curriculum development that might be described as more open to disagreement on what defines them.

Of the last seven ranks (49-55) curriculum practices, the professors' ratings showed that there were three curriculum practices in the domain of curriculum policy and two curriculum practices in the domain of curriculum development. Curriculum practices in domains of curriculum design, curriculum policy, curriculum policy, curriculum policy, curriculum evaluation, curriculum development, and curriculum development were ranked   49, 50, 51, 52, 53.5, 53.5, and 55 respectively. The results indicate that the professors assigned lower rankings to practices in curriculum policy and curriculum development. These findings suggest that there is less agreement about the importance of these domains among the Professors of Curriculum.

Table 4.13
Summary of Curriculum Practices Assigned to Ranks 1 - 5 and 50 - 55* by the Midwest Teachers (*MWTCHR*), the Southeast Teachers (*SETCHR*), and the Professors of Curriculum (*PROFCURR*).

Rank   MWTCHR
1. Integrates content and learning experiences. (CD)
2.5 Guides program development for individual students. (DE)**

Table 4.13 contd

2.5 Indicates instructional strategies to be utilized. (DE)
4. Identifies the strengths of curriculum content. (CE)
5. Integrates careful planning. (DE)**
50. Analyzes resisting and supporting forces. (CR)***
50. Communicates with local and state government agencies. (PO)+
50. Influences the control of the curriculum. (PO)
52 Determines the ends of education. (CP)
53. Elaborates on the theory of curriculum. (CP)
54. Describes past curriculum thought and practices. (CH)
55. Reflecting upon schools of thought including: perennialism; essentialism; progressivism; reconstructionism; and existentialism. (CP) ***

Rank   SETCHR
1. Provides information about the effectiveness of the curriculum. (CE)
2. Determines if objectives have been met. (CE)
3. Integrates careful planning. (DE) **
4.5 Develops curriculum guides. (CD)
4.5 Guides program development for individual students. (DE) **
51. Mandates school goals. (PO) ++
52.5 Reflecting upon schools of thought including: perennialism; essentialism; progressivism; reconstructionism; and existentialism. (CP) ***
52.5 Analyzes resisting and supporting forces. (CR) ***
54. Interprets past curriculum practice. (CH)
55. Advances hypotheses and assumptions of the field. (CR)

Rank   PROFCURR
1. Suggests a view of society and students in relationship to education. (CR)
2. 5 Determines an orientation to curriculum. (CR)
2.5 Permits curriculum ideas to function. (DE)
4. Attempts to integrate theory and practice. (CF)
5. Describes past curriculum throuht and practices. (CH)
50. States what ought to be taught. (PO)
51. Communicates with local and state government agencies. (PO)+
52. Mandates school goals. (PO) ++
53.5 Measures discrepancies between predetermined objectives and outcomes. (CD)

Table 4.13 contd

53.5 Develops curriculum guides. (CD)
55. Develops school grants. (CD)

Notes:
* = Three practices tied for rank order 49, therefore, only ranks 51-55 are shown.
* *= Ranked by Midwest and Southeast teachers as one of the first five most important curriculum practices
** * = Ranked by Midwest and Southeast teachers among the first five least important curriculum practices
+ = Ranked by Midwest teachers and the Professors of Curriculum among the first five least important curriculum practices
++ = Ranked by Southeast teachers and the Professors of Curriculum among the first five least important curriculum practices

---

Table 4.13 provides a summary of the curriculum practices that were ranked 1-5 and 50-55 by the Midwest and Southeast teachers and the Professors of Curriculum. Overall, there is no agreement between the professors and the teachers regarding the curriculum practices to which they assigned the first five ranks and designated as most important. The Midwest and Southeast teachers selected and assigned two of the same practices (guides program development for individual students and integrated careful planning), both in the domain of curriculum design as one of the first five rank ordered statements. An overview of ranks 50-55 revealed that the Midwest and Southeast teachers rated two of the same practices, one in curriculum philosophy (reflecting upon schools of thought including: perennialism; essentialism; progressivism; reconstructionism; and existentialism), and one in curriculum research (analyzes resisting and supporting forces) among the least important. The Midwest teachers and the professors agreed that one practice in curriculum policy (communicates with local and state government agencies) was the least important practice. The Southeast teachers and the professors agreed that one curriculum practice in curriculum policy (mandates school goals) was among the least important.

Table 4.14
Summary of the Total Mean Responses for the Importance of Curriculum Practices within the Domains of Curriculum by the Midwest Teachers, Southeast Teachers, and Professors of Curriculum

DOMAINS OF CURRICULUM

TOTAL - ITEM MEANS

MWTCHR (N = 48)	SETCHR (N = 37)	PROFCURR (N = 51)

I. CURRICULUM PHILOSOPHY

3.2743	3.3919	4.1765

II. CURRICULUM THEORY

3.7167	3.5459	3.7647

III. CURRICULUM RESEARCH

3.6208	3.4162	3.7294

IV. CURRICULUM HISTORY

3.4479	3.3176	3.9657

V. CURRICULUM DEVELOPMENT

3.6632	3.6126	3.3007

VI. CURRICULUM DESIGN

3.9494	3.8919	3.5994

VII. CURRICULUM EVALUATION

3.8157	3.6778	3.1463

VIII. CURRICULUM POLICY

3.4833	3.4703	2.9608

IX. CURRICULUM AS A FIELD OF STUDY

3.7083	3.5608	4.0539

Table 4.14 contd

Notes: <u>Importance</u>
                          5 = very important
                          4 = fairly important
                          3 = some importance
                          2 = fairly unimportant
                          1 = very unimportant

Table 4.14 presents a summary of the total means responses related to the importance of the domains by the teachers and professors. Taken as a whole, each of the domain subscales was rated of some importance except for three instances. The Professors of Curriculum rated the domain of curriculum policy as fairly unimportant. In contrast, they rated the domains of curriculum philosophy and curriculum as a field of study as fairly important.

An overview of the rank order total item means revealed a natural break between the total mean scores of 3.81 and 3.76. An analysis of the rank ordered total means scores of 3.76 or higher showed that the Midwest teachers rated two domains in this range (curriculum design (3.95) and curriculum evaluation (3.82)). The Southeast teachers rated only one domain as 3.76 or higher (curriculum design (3.89)). The total item means for domains rated as 3.75 or higher by Professors of Curriculum were four: curriculum philosophy (4.18); curriculum theory (3.76); curriculum history (3.97); and curriculum as a field of study (4.05). Domain scores of 3.76 or higher were on the higher end of the category designated as of some importance and approached the category designated as fairly important.

Table 4.15
Mean Responses for the Importance and Coverage of Curriculum Practices within the Domains of Curriculum by Professors of Curriculum

DOMAINS OF CURRICULUM

TOTAL-ITEM MEANS
I. CURRICULUM PHILOSOPHY

Importance   Coverage
4.1765*   4.2190*

Curriculum Practice

1. Reflecting upon schools of thought including: perennialism; essentialism; progressivism; reconstructionism; and existentialism.
4.0588   3.9412

2. Determines the ends of education.
3.9412   3.9608

3. Determines an orientation to curriculum.
4.3529   4.4902

4. Suggests a view of society and students in relationship to education.
4.3922   4.2745

5. States the purposes of education.
4.1176   4.1961

6. Elaborates on the theory of curriculum.
4.1961   4.4510

Table 4.15 contd

II. CURRICULUM THEORY
Importance   Coverage
3.7647*   3.5137*

Curriculum Practice

7. Creates statements that give meaning to a school curriculum.
3.9608   3.9020

8. Uses techniques of science and logic to present a systematic view of phenomena.
3.4314   3.1373

9. Deals with structuring knowledge.
4.1569   3.9412

10. Identifies how students learn.
3.4902   2.8039

11. Uses principles and rules to study curriculum.
3.7843   3.7843

Table 4.15 contd

III. CURRICULUM RESEARCH

<u>Importance</u>   <u>Coverage</u>
3.7294*   3.5961*

<u>Curriculum Practice</u>
12. Analyzes resisting and supporting forces.
3.7451   3.6275

13. Advances hypotheses and assumptions of the field.
4.1765   4.1373

14. Uses systematic inquiry for the purpose of solving a particular problem.
3.2157   3.0980

15. Analyzes steps to be taken in problem solving.
3.2941   3.1373

16. Focuses on research and/or inquiry of curriculum.
4.2157   3.9804

IV. CURRICULUM HISTORY
<u>Importance</u>   <u>Coverage</u>
3.9657*   4.0147*

<u>Curriculum Practice</u>
17. Describes past curriculum thought and practices.
4.2745   4.3725

18. Interprets past curriculum practice.
3.8627   4.1176

19. Provides a chronology of important events in curriculum.
3.7059   3.7059

20. Examines forces that inhibit curriculum innovations.
4.0196   3.8627

Table 4.15 contd

V. CURRICULUM DEVELOPMENT

Importance   Coverage
3.3007*   2.9706*

Curriculum Practice

21. Develops curriculum guides.
2.4510   1.9804

22. Develops school grants.
2.0784   1.6078

23. Determines procedures necessary for a curriculum plan.
3.4510   2.9216

24. Addresses questions of who will be involved in curriculum construction.
3.9804   3.6471

25. Integrates content and learning experiences.
3.9608   3.5294

26. Decides on nature and organization of curriculum.
3.8824   4.1373

Table 4.15 contd

VI. CURRICULUM DESIGN
<u>Importance</u>   <u>Coverage</u>
3.5994*   3.2241*

<u>Curriculum Practice</u>

27. Attempts to define what subject matter will be used.
3.5882   3.2353

28. Guides program development for individual students.
3.4118   2.7059

29. Selects subject matter and learning experiences.
3.6667   3.2549

30. Establishes the primary focus of subject matter.
3.7059   3.4118

31. Permits curriculum ideas to function.
4.3529   4.2157

32. Integrates careful planning.
3.6853   3.2549

33. Indicates instructional strategies to be utilized.
2.7843   2.4902

Table 4.15 contd

VII. CURRICULUM EVALUATION

<u>Importance</u>   <u>Coverage</u>
3.4163*   3.0649*

<u>Curriculum Practice</u>
34. Determines what changes took place as a result of the curriculum.
4.0980   3.5490

35. Provides information about the effectiveness of the curriculum.
3.7451   3.5686

36. Determines whether actions yielded predicted results.
3.2745   2.7647

37. Determines if objectives have been met.
3.4706   2.9412

38. Offers suggestions for curriculum modification.
3.7647   3.2745

39. Measures discrepancies between predetermined objectives and outcomes.
2.4510   2.1373

40. Judges worth of instructional methods and materials.
3.1765   2.6667

41. Determines desired outcomes of instruction.
2.9412   3.2157

42. Improves curriculum programs.
3.5098   3.1569

43. Determines effectiveness of curriculum content.
3.3922   3.1765

44. Ascertains whether outcomes are the result of the curriculum.
3.1765   2.7843

Table 4.15 contd
VII. CURRICULUM EVALUATION

<u>Curriculum Practice</u>

45. Determines criteria to measure success of curriculum plan.
3.6667   3.0588

46. Identifies the strengths of curriculum content.
3.7451   3.5490

VIII. CURRICULUM POLICY

<u>Importance</u>   <u>Coverage</u>
2.9608*   2.8196*

<u>Curriculum Practice</u>

47. Influences control of the curriculum.
3.9608   3.7059

48. Recommends what learning experience to include.
3.0196   2.6863

49. Mandates school goals.
2.4706   2.5098

50. States what ought to be taught.
2.7647   2.8431

51. Communicates with local and state government agencies.
2.5882   2.3529

IX. CURRICULUM AS A FIELD OF STUDY
<u>Importance</u>   <u>Coverage</u>
4.0539*   3.8529*

<u>Curriculum Practice</u>

52. Promotes curriculum planning and implementation.
3.6863   3.4706

Table 4.15 contd

IX. CURRICULUM AS A FIELD OF STUDY
<u>Curriculum Practice</u>

53. Organizes patterns and structures of curriculum.
4.1765   3.9608

54. Attempts to integrate theory and practice.
4.3137   4.0196

55. Analyzes structures of curriculum.
4.0392   3.9608

Notes: * = Total mean for the domain subscale
       <u>Importance</u>

               5 = very important
               4 = fairly important
               3 = some importance
               2 = fairly unimportant
               1 = very unimportant

       <u>Coverage</u>

               5 = very great extent
               4 = great extent
               3 = some extent
               2 = little extent
               1 = very little extent

Coverage of Curriculum Practices per Mean Scores

Mean scores in the range of 1-2, denoted that items were covered to a very little extent. Mean scores in the range of 2-3, denoted that items were covered to a little extent, scores greater in the range 3-4 indicated that items were covered to some extent. Items with mean scores greater than 4 demonstrated that items were covered to a great extent, as per the Likert scale. Table 4.15 shows the mean response for the importance of and coverage for each curriculum practice as rated by the Professors of Curriculum as well as the total mean for each domain subscale.

As for coverage, two curriculum practices were rated as covered to a very little extent, fourteen were rated covered to a little extent, twenty-nine were judged to be covered some extent, and ten were rated covered to a great extent. Each of the curriculum practices were assessed by nonparametric correlational techniques to determine the strength of association between the ratings of importance of curriculum practices and the extent to which the curriculum practices were covered in the selected textbook.

Table 4.16
Spearman Correlation Coefficients for Importance of Curriculum Practices with Coverage of Curriculum Practices within the Domains of Curriculum by Professors of Curriculum (N = 51)

DOMAINS OF CURRICULUM

I. CURRICULUM PHILOSOPHY
<u>Coefficient</u>   <u>N pairs</u>   <u>Significance</u>

<u>Curriculum Practice</u>

1. Reflecting upon schools of thought including: perennialism; essentialism; progressivism; reconstructionism; and existentialism.
.4526   48   .001***

2. Determines the ends of education.
.7049   49   .001***

Table 4.16 contd
<u>Coefficient</u>   <u>N pairs</u>   <u>Significance</u>

<u>Curriculum Practice</u>

3. Determines an orientation to curriculum.
.5911   48   .001***

4. Suggests a view of society and students in relationship to education.
.4487   50   .001***

5. States the purposes of education.
.7251   50   .001***

6. Elaborates on the theory of curriculum.
.4399   50   .001***

II. CURRICULUM THEORY
<u>Coefficient</u>   <u>N pairs</u>   <u>Significance</u>

<u>Curriculum Practice</u>

7. Creates statements that give meaning to a school curriculum.
.6695   49   .001***

8. Uses techniques of science and logic to present a systematic view of phenomena.
.4417   46   .001***

9. Deals with structuring knowledge.
.6097   48   .001***

10. Identifies how students learn.
.2799   50   .05*

11. Uses principles and rules to study curriculum.
.5780   48   .001***

Table 4.16 contd

III. CURRICULUM RESEARCH
Coefficient   N pairs   Significance

Curriculum Practice

12. Analyzes resisting and supporting forces.
.3848   49   .01**

13. Advances hypotheses and assumptions of the field.
.3757   50   .01**

14. Uses systematic inquiry for the purpose of solving a particular problem.
.5778   50   .001***

15. Analyzes steps to be taken in problem solving.
.8349   47   .001***

16. Focuses on research and/or inquiry of curriculum.
.6519   49   .001***

IV. CURRICULUM HISTORY
Coefficient   N pairs   Significance

Curriculum Practice

17. Describes past curriculum thought and practices.
.7001   48   .001***

18. Interprets past curriculum practice.
.6873   50   .001***

19. Provides a chronology of important events in curriculum.
.7038   50   .001***

20. Examines forces that inhibit curriculum innovations.
.7661   48   .001***

Table 4.16 contd
V. CURRICULUM DEVELOPMENT
<u>Coefficient</u>   <u>N pairs</u>   <u>Significance</u>

<u>Curriculum Practice</u>

21. Develops curriculum guides.
.6286   49   .001***

22. Develops school grants.
.5903   49   .001***

23. Determines procedures necessary for a curriculum plan.
.6773   50   .001***

24. Addresses questions of who will be involved in curriculum construction.
.6206   50   .001***

25. Integrates content and learning experiences.
.5430   48   .001***

26. Decides on nature and organization of curriculum.
.3629   48   .01**

VI. CURRICULUM DESIGN
<u>Coefficient</u>   <u>N pairs</u>   <u>Significance</u>

<u>Curriculum Practice</u>

27. Attempts to define what subject matter will be used.
.4870   48   .001***

28. Guides program development for individual students.
.6428   48   .001***

29. Selects subject matter and learning experiences.
.5743   47   .001***

30. Establishes the primary focus of subject matter.
.6986   47   .001***

Table 4.16 contd
VI. CURRICULUM DESIGN
<u>Coefficient</u>   <u>N pairs</u>   <u>Significance</u>

<u>Curriculum Practice</u>

31. Permits curriculum ideas to function.
.7194   47   .001***
Table 4.16 contd

32. Integrates careful planning.
.5302   48   .001***

33. Indicates instructional strategies to be utilized.
.5126   50   .001***

VII. CURRICULUM EVALUATION
<u>Coefficient</u>   <u>N pairs</u>   <u>Significance</u>

<u>Curriculum Practice</u>

34. Determines what changes took place as a result
of the curriculum.
.3076   47   .05*

35. Provides information about the effectiveness of
the curriculum.
.4082   47   .01**

36. Determines whether actions yielded
predicted results.
.4835   47   .001***

37. Determines if objectives have been met.
.6033   47   .001***

38. Offers suggestions for curriculum modification.
.5981   48   .001***

39. Measures discrepancies between predetermined objectives and
outcomes.
.6841   50   .001***

Table 4.16 contd
VII. CURRICULUM EVALUATION

Coefficient   N pairs   Significance

Curriculum Practice

40. Judges worth of instructional methods and materials.
.5012   49   .001***

41. Determines desired outcomes of instruction.
.6196   48   .001***
Table 4.16 contd

42. Improves curriculum programs.
.6979   49   .001***

43. Determines effectiveness of curriculum content.
.3765   48   .01**

44. Ascertains whether outcomes are the result of the curriculum
.5050   48   .001***

45. Determines criteria to measure success of curriculum plan.
.4335   49   .001***

46. Identifies the strengths of curriculum content.
.5789   49   .001***

VIII. CURRICULUM POLICY

Coefficient   N pairs   Significance

Curriculum Practice

47. Influences control of the curriculum.
.8301   48   .001***

48. Recommends what learning experience to include.
.5489   50   .001***

49. Mandates school goals.
.5897   47   .001***

Table 4.16 contd
VIII. CURRICULUM POLICY

<u>Coefficient</u>   <u>N pairs</u>   <u>Significance</u>

<u>Curriculum Practice</u>

50. States what ought to be taught.
.5695   49   .001***

51. Communicates with local and state government agencies.
.5276   48   .001***

52. Promotes curriculum planning and implementation.
.6715   49   .001***

53. Organizes patterns and structures of curriculum.
.5639   49   .001***

54. Attempts to integrate theory and practice.
.7305   50   .001***

55. Analyzes structures of curriculum.
.6669   49   .001***

Notes: * = Significance < .05
          ** = Significance < .01
          *** = Significane < .001

Table 4.16 shows the correlation coefficients computed for each the curriculum practices and representative subscales within the domains of curriculum. As indicated by the results, there were significant levels of agreement between the ratings of the importance of curriculum practices and coverage of the corresponding curriculum practices within the domains of curriculum. Forty-eight items evidenced a Spearman correlation coefficient significant at < .001 level. Two items were found to be significant at the <.01 level. Five items were significant at the < .05 level.

Table 4.17

Spearman Correlation Coefficients for Importance of Curriculum Practices with Coverage of Curriculum by Subscales within the Domains of Curriculum by Professors of Curriculum (N = 51)

DOMAINS OF CURRICULUM	Coefficient	N	Significance
Curriculum Philosophy	.7571	50	.001***
Curriculum Evaluation	.5689	50	.001***
Curriculum Design	.6050	50	.001***
Curriculum Theory	.7247	50	.001***
Curriculum Policy	.6571	50	.001***
Curriculum History	.8348	50	.001***
Curriculum Development	.5746	50	.001***
Curriculum Research	.6505	50	.001***
Curriculum as a Field of Study	.7264	50	.001***

Notes: *** = Significance < .001

Table 4.17 shows the correlation coefficient computed for each subscale with the domains of curriculum. As indicated in Table 4.17 there were significant levels of agreement between the ratings of the importance and coverage of the corresponding subscales within the domains of curriculum. In fact, the Spearman correlation coefficients for each of the nine subscales were significant at the < .001 level. Taken as a whole, there were significant levels of agreement between the professors ratings of importance and coverage for both the domains and the related curriculum practices.

Table 4.18
Summary of Frequency Responses to Most Influential Textbooks in Curriculum by Order of Rank

<u>Author</u>	<u>Textbook Title</u>	
<u>Votes</u>	<u>Percent</u>	<u>Rank</u>
<u>Publisher</u>	<u>Date of Publication</u>	
Schubert,W.	*Curriculum: Perspectives, Paradigm, and Possibility*	
13	25.5	1
Macmillan	1986	
Tanner, D. &		
Tanner, L.	*Curriculum Development: Theory into Practice*	
9	17.8	2.5
Macmillan	1980	
Zais, R.	*Curriculum: Principles and Foundations*	
9	17.8	2.5
Crowell	1976	
Goodlad, J.	*A Place Called School*	
6	11.8	4
McGraw-Hill	1984	
Pinar, W.	*Contemporary Curriculum Discourses*	
5	9.8	5
Gorsuch & Scarisbrick	1988	
Eisner, E.	*The Educational Imagination*	
4	7.8	6
Macmillan	1985	
Eisner, E. &		
Vallance, E.	*Conflicting Conceptions of Curriculum*	
3	5.9	7
McCutchan	1974	

Author	Textbook Title		
Votes	Percent	Rank	
Publisher			Date of Publication

Table 4.18 contd

Goodlad, J.	Curriculum Inquiry		
1	2.0	8	
McGraw Hill			1979

Apple, M.	Ideology and Curriculum		
0	0.0	10	
Routledge & Paul			1986

Giroux, H.			
Penna, A. &			
Pinar, W.	Curriculum and Instruction		
0	0.0	10	
McCutchan			1981

Kliebard, H.	The Struggle for the American		
	Curriculum (1893-1958)		
0	0.0	10	
Routledge & Paul			1986

Pinar, W.	Curriculum Theorizing: The Reconceptualists		
0	0.0	10	
McCutchan			1975

With respect to research question five, Table 4.18 presents a descriptive summary regarding the most influential textbooks in curriculum. Schubert's *Curriculum: Perspectives, Paradigms, and Possibilities* was selected by 13 respondents, or 25.5%. Both Tanner and Tanner's *Curriculum Development: Theory into Practice* and Zais' *Curriculum: Principles and Foundation* were selected by 9 or 17.8% of the respondents.

Goodlad's *A Place Called School* was selected by 6 or 11.8% of the respondents and ranked fourth. The selections for rank orders five through eight respectively were: Pinar's *Contemporary Curriculum Discourses* (N = 5 or 9.8%); Eisner's *The Educational Imagination* (N =4, 7.8%); Eisner and Vallance's *Conflicting Conceptions of Curriculum* (N = 3, 5.9%); and Goodlad's *Curriculum Inquiry* (N = 1, 2.0%). Four textbooks were not selected by any of the respondents and tied for rank order ten including: Apple's *Ideology and Curriculum;* Giroux, Penna and Pinar's *Curriculum and Instruction;* Kliebard's *The Struggle for the American Curriculum (1893-1958);* and Pinar's *Curriculum Theorizing: The Reconceptualists.*

Summary and Analysis of Findings

The findings revealed very strong correlations between the ratings of the importance and coverage of curriculum practices within textbooks. This supports the notion that Professors of Curriculum selected textbooks that were consistent with their viewpoints regarding domains of curriculum. Because of the strong agreement between importance and coverage, the findings suggest that there exists a set of curriculum practices that represent what the investigator defined as domains of curriculum.

---

[1] The original criterion for selecting a textbook as most influential was designated as 20%. However, only 8 textbooks met this criterion. Four textbooks were cited by 15.8% of the respondents and were tied for rank order ten. The list was extended to a total of twelve textbooks to include the textbooks tied for rank order ten.

[2] Based on consultation with Drs. Jack Kavanagh and Ronald Morgan, who teach advanced statistics and research at Loyola University of Chicago, it is agreed that there was no statistical test to determine the veracity or falsity of a related null hypothesis. Therefore, the results will be discussed by descriptive analysis.

[3] As previously described, the six categories originally designated for the year in which professors earned their doctorates were collasped into two categories, category 1, (1951-1970) and category two, (1971-1990).

[4] As previously described, the five categories originally designated for the geographical region of the institution where the professors earned their doctorate was collasped into two categories, category one, East and category two, Midwest.

CHAPTER V

CONCLUSIONS, IMPLICATIONS AND RECOMMENDATIONS

The overall purpose of this study was to establish a quantifiable knowledge base of curriculum domains and related practices. In addition, an attempt was made to determine if the Professors of Curriculum would select textbooks that were consistent with the viewpoints they identified as most important regarding the domains of curriculum.

The results of this study showed that the Professors of Curriculum identified twelve influential textbooks in curriculum. Overall, the findings showed that the Midwest teacher group showed high levels of homogeneity in their ratings of the importance of curriculum domains and moderate levels to high practices of homogeneity with respect to curriculum practices. The Southeast teacher group demonstrated moderate to high levels of internal consistency in their ratings of importance of curriculum domains and low to moderate ratings of the importance for the curriculum practices. There was significant agreement among the professors concerning their ratings of the importance and coverage of curriculum practices within the domains of curriculum. Within the context of this study, a knowledge base of curriculum practices was identified.

This chapter begins with a description of what has taken place up to this point. Secondly, a summary of the findings regarding the professors' selections of textbooks in the textbook and domains survey is presented. Then, their ratings of the relative importance of curriculum practices in the domains is presented. Thirdly, the test results for each research question are described. This chapter concludes with a discussion of the unanticipated limitations that emerged in the course of this study, recommendations for future research, and a summary.

Background Information of the Study

In accord with the purposes of this study, the knowledge base of curriculum was described in terms of **domains of curriculum** and related behaviors and activities, that is, **curriculum practices,** that defined the domains. A survey instrument was developed. The domains and related curriculum practices were quantified through formal reliability and validity procedures. A group of Midwest and Southeast teachers rated the importance of the curriculum practices for the purposes of establishing reliability. A selection of influential textbooks in the field of curriculum published between 1970-1990 was undertaken; twelve textbooks were identified by Professors of Curriculum. By means of the domains survey approach, these survey items were further shown to demonstrate internal consistency and agreement between their ratings of importance and extent of text coverage by the Professors of Curriculum.

Professors of Curriculum Selections in the Textbook Survey

One aspect of this study was to determine if the Professors of Curriculum would identify an agreed upon listing of the most influential curriculum textbooks.   The results showed that the Professors of Curriculum identified twelve influential textbooks in the field of curriculum published between 1970-1990. Schubert's *Curriculum: Perspectives, Paradigm, and Possibility* was selected most frequently in the open ended survey. Eisners' *The Educational Imagination* and Tanner & Tanner's *Curriculum Development: Theory into Practice* were ranked two, and three respectively.

An assessment of the potential of significant relationships between demographic variables and the professors' textbook selections revealed that the professors' preferences were not significantly influenced by these variables. Other criteria that might have suggested reasons for their selections were not elicited. However, several inferences can be offered based on the findings.

The results suggest that these textbooks were influential and perhaps widely recognized, but do not imply that they are widely used or regarded as textbooks. The results also do not offer information that suggests which textbook is most often purchased by curriculum professors or students of curriculum.

In spite of the academic orientation of the Professors of Curriculum, the findings suggest that this sample of the professors were not favorably disposed to traditional textbooks or that they had a anti-textbook orientation. In noting the Apple's *Ideology and Curriculum* (rank order 7) and Pinar's *Curriculum Theorizing: The Reconceptualists* and *Contemporary Curriculum Discourses* (rank order 5.5 and 10 respectively) citations, it might be inferred that a larger segment of the sample has a reconceptualized philosophy of curriculum. Furthermore, while the textbooks shown in Table 4.1 may have had impact on the academic study of curriculum they may have had little influence on curriculum in practice and had only minor if any impact upon the way in which curriculum is written about and studied in university curriculum programs.[5] To make any assumptions about the usage or importance of the textbooks shown in Table 4.1 would be precarious because the sample population size is too small to render generalizations.

Finally, it should be noted that the findings in Table 4.1 are the perceptions of the Professors of Curriculum; they are not necessarily generalizable to other populations. Additional research that includes qualitative descriptions of the rationale for textbook selections, as well as different respondents groups, e.g., other professional boards, curriculum department chairs, or directors of teacher education programs in private and public sector universities, along with the Professors of Curriculum, should be undertaken in future studies in order to provide comparative data.

Professors of Curriculum Textbook Selections in the Domains Survey

Schubert's *Curriculum: Perspectives. Paradigm, & Possibilities* was selected most frequently in both the close ended and open ended surveys. This finding suggests that his textbook was influential, but does not necessarily imply that it is widely used and regarded as a textbook in the field of curriculum. It would be problematic to make any assumptions about the usage or importance of the textbooks shown in Table 4.18

because the sample population is too small to render generalizations. The findings presented in Table 4.18 are solely the perceptions of the Professors of Curriculum and as previously stated, are not necessarily generalizable to other populations. Collectively, Schubert's text, Tanner & Tanner's *Curriculum: Theory into Practice,* and Zais' *Curriculum: Principles and Foundations* were cited by 60.7% or (N=31) of the professors who responded to the close ended survey. These results indicated that Professors of Curriculum were most familiar with these three textbooks. Other texts listed in rank order were: Goodlad's *A Place Called School* (N=6, 11.8%); Pinar's *Contemporary Curriculum Discourses* (N=5, 9.5%); Eisner's *The Educational Imagination* (N=4, 7.8%); and Eisner & Vallance's *Conflicting Conceptions of Curriculum* (N=3, 5.9%). Selection votes assigned to these four textbooks accounted for 35.3% or (N=18) of the close ended survey responses. Perhaps these textbooks were cited less frequently than the Schubert, Tanner & Tanner, and Zais' textbooks because the professors were less familiar with them.

It should be noted that there was similarity in the rank order listings of textbooks in the open and close ended surveys. The Schubert, Eisner, and Tanner & Tanner textbooks were ranked one to three respectively in the textbook survey. In the domains survey, the Schubert, Tanner & Tanner, and Zais textbooks were ranked one through three respectively. The differences in the rank ordering of the textbooks was probably related to the nature of the survey tasks. In the open ended (textbook) survey, the professors were asked to list up to ten books without indicating rank. In the close ended domains survey, the professors were instructed to select only one textbook.

Summary of Findings Related to the Importance of Curriculum Practices

With respect to the teachers and professors ratings of the importance of curriculum practices, of the original 55 items, 47 curriculum practices (85%) remained at the conclusion of this study. These items demonstrated acceptable levels of internal consistency, and had an alpha coefficient of at least .20. Only three acceptable items remained for the domains of curriculum development, (determines procedures necessary for a curriculum plan, integrates content and learning experiences, and decides on the nature and organization of curriculum). Two curriculum practices remained in curriculum policy (mandates school goals and states what ought to be taught). Since the established minimum number of items for a subscale was four, the under representation for these domains represents a limitation of the final survey instrument. The contribution of a subscale of less than four items to the overall meaning of the instrument is somewhat questionable. This suggests that perhaps the curriculum practices or the subscale were unimportant, or that neither were a priority consideration for one or more of the respondents, namely the Midwest teachers, Southeast teachers, or Professors of Curriculum.

With respect to ratings of the curriculum practices and the selection of textbooks in the closed ended survey sent to the Professors of Curriculum, it should be indicated that perhaps the curriculum practices statements in the survey might have suggested a view of curriculum that was not applicable to books such as Giroux, Penna & Pinar's *Curriculum and Instruction.* Pinar's *Curriculum Theorizing: The Reconceptualists* and Apple's *Ideology and Curriculum.*

Implications of the Study

A summary of the findings in relationship to the research questions indicates that for **research question 1**, a listing of twelve textbooks published between 1970-1990 and identified as most influential was established. Regarding **research question 2,** an assessment of the potential significance of five demographic variables regarding the Professors textbooks responses to the textbook survey showed that these variables did not significantly influence the Professors of Curriculum selections of the most influential curriculum textbooks. The findings concerning **research question 3,** showed that the Midwest teachers demonstrated moderate to high levels of homogeneity in their ratings of importance of curriculum practices and the domains of curriculum. With respect to **research question 4**, the Southeast teacher group demonstrated low to high levels of homogeneity in their ratings of importance of curriculum practices and domains of curriculum. The results concerning **research question 5,** showed that there were significant levels of agreement among the Professors of Curriculum in their ratings of importance and coverage of the domains of curriculum and their related practices. Additionally, a quantifiable knowledge base of fifty-five curriculum practices and nine domains of curriculum practices was established within the overall context of this study.

Based upon findings of the mean responses of the ratings for importance of curriculum practices as indicated by the Professors of

Curriculum, it might be inferred that practices in the domains of curriculum philosophy, curriculum theory, curriculum research, curriculum history, and curriculum as a field of study are more entrenched and traditional. Perhaps the professors regard these practices as foundations and have a better notion of what activities or behaviors describe these domains. These findings also suggest that there is less agreement among the Professors of Curriculum about the activities (behaviors) that describe the domains of curriculum development, curriculum design, and curriculum evaluation.

In contrast, the teacher groups tended to rate and rank the importance of domain practices within curriculum development and curriculum design higher than the Professors of Curriculum. There appears to be less agreement among the teachers regarding the importance of curriculum practices in the domains of curriculum philosophy, curriculum history, and curriculum policy.

Perhaps the more entrenched and traditional curriculum practices have greater utility for professors than for practitioners. If this is the case, it might be necessary to revisit post secondary programs of education and re-examine the synchronicity between training and practical applications in the world of actual curriculum applications.

These findings have both practical implications as well as implications for future research. The Professors' of Curriculum ratings of the importance and coverage of curriculum practices in the domains suggests evidence of a consensus between the professors' theoretical and philosophical beliefs and their textbook selections.

As stated in the introduction, the curriculum practices (items) were selected by the investigator's synthesis of curriculum textbooks published between 1970 to 1990 and are limited to the domains of curriculum. These items are representative of the kinds of activities in which curriculum workers, that is, teachers, curriculum coordinators, teacher education and curriculum professors engage in while doing curriculum related tasks. Perhaps they will be useful in clarifying a knowledge base of tasks that guide program development or assist practitioners in identifying professional and educational needs.

Hopefully, the knowledge base of curriculum practices identified in this research project will influence the design and delivery of professional education programs; help define program purpose; and provide education with a focus for thinking about curriculum and instructional techniques. These practices might be useful in formulating a framework for professional education, establishing structure for making informed decisions, evaluating program delivery, or identifying organizational disparities. They might also be useful in assisting education to define goals, identify organizing themes, and develop program models.

The procedures used in this study might have utility for other branches of education such as administration and supervision as well as the social sciences including psychology and sociology. The process of identifying domains of curriculum occurred by a content analysis of curriculum textbooks published between 1970-1990. This procedure of identifying classical topical categories (domains) could be extended to all curriculum books published since 1900, or a compendium of important curriculum practices could be ascertained through survey analysis of the Professors of Curriculum and department chairs of doctoral curriculum programs throughout the U.S. In the same connection, the domains and curriculum practices might have been selected from the textbooks identified in the textbook survey by the Professors of Curriculum and other respondent groups and subsequently categorized and validated by a group of expert judges. A flow chart summary of the procedures used in this study appears below:

1. IDENTIFY DOMAINS
2. DEFINE DOMAINS
3. CATEGORIZE DOMAIN PRACTICES
4. SELECT TEXTBOOKS
5. ESTABLISH RELIABILITY - (TEACHER GROUP 1)
6. ESTABLISH RELIABILITY - (TEACHER GROUP 2)
7. ESTABLISH RELIABILITY
   (PROFESSORS OF CURRICULUM)
8. ASSESS AGREEMENT BETWEEN THE IMPORTANCE AND
   COVERAGE OF CURRICULUM PRACTICES

Textbooks play an influential role in how curriculum is used, taught, and understood. They significantly impact on how learners interact with, think about and/or interpret subject matter. Textbooks also highlight the degree of consensus or fragmentation within a discipline. They provide direction of the field as a subject matter entity and are instrumental in guiding students' mastery of the fundamental structures of disciplines. Curriculum textbooks can perpetuate the status quo of the field, reflect controversy within the field, or highlight emergent trends by analyzing or advocating the ideas that practitioners espouse. Curriculum textbooks offer ideas about curriculum content that might influence curriculum systems and decision making in local school districts. A content analysis of textbooks can be a source for defining knowledge bases.

Using curriculum textbooks as a source for defining the activities and behaviors that curriculum workers use while engaged in actual teaching situations and observing the frequency and conditions under which these behaviors occur in classrooms or other educational situations, might provide curriculum scholars with another dimension for defining a theory of curriculum. The content analysis of curriculum textbooks used in this study and the ratings of the practices within the domains suggests that there is some measurable consensus within the field. The ideas discussed in this research study lend themselves to the notion of theory building activities advocated by McCutcheon (1988) that involves using empirical methods to confirm or disconfirm relationships, highlighting relationships between variables, or questioning the plausibility of predictability between events, experiences or phenomena. The processes used in this study and the conceptual framework also coincide with Johnson's (1967) recommendation to identify desired outputs in behavioral terms that would serve as the foundation for theory building. If it is our intention is to articulate any type of paradigm in curriculum that has predictability, then it is necessary that we reach some consensus about the definition and operationalization of key constructs, questions, and concepts.

Potential Limitations of this Research Study

As with any research, the results should be viewed within the context of the parameters of the study.

1. This study restricted the professors' textbook selections to books published between 1970 to 1990.

2. It should be noted that the curriculum practices comprising the domains of curriculum were selected independently of the textbooks.

3. This investigation did not eliminate textbook authors who were members of the Professors of Curriculum.

4. This study did not utilize an alternate mechanism to validate the Professors of Curriculum selections.

Recommendations

Future researchers should seek to:

1. Utilize an inductive process that involves studying the frequency and conditions under which these behaviors occur and compare the results with these deductive findings.

2. Apply the methods and procedures similar to those used in this investigation and determine whether other social science disciplines such as psychology, sociology have an established knowledge base of practices.

3. Implement a method of systematically identifying topical categories in undergraduate or graduate level curriculum textbooks, classical books or content area textbooks to determine if specific domains of knowledge exist.

4. Identify the most influential textbooks in curriculum without an epochal parameter (i.e., only textbooks published between 1970-1990).

5. Utlilize additional means to validate the professors' responses in the textbook survey. Comparing the Professors identification of the most influential textbooks to sales figures reported by major publishers would be an objective means to validate the professors' selections.

Conclusions

By themselves, the 55 curriculum practices represent the important behaviors of curriculum specialists. Although no educational program can be devised which will encompass all agreed upon knowledge, it is essential to determine and operationalize what practices are needed to improve the curriculum process. In order to engage in dialogue or inquiry about curriculum domains, it is important that these constructs be defined in the same way. It seems that empirical investigations are needed to clarify domains if we hope to move discussions beyond the linguistic and metaphorical levels.

The behaviors and activities listed in Table 4.9 help establish behaviors or criteria for the emerging roles of the curriculum specialist. This compendium of practices might have utility as an evaluation tool for principals. Principals might use this list to assess teachers' instructional skills and identify their methodological strengths and weaknesses. The curriculum practices serve as criteria or requirements for graduate study involving curriculum certification, staff development for curriculum specialists, and for making curriculum decisions from many levels--school, district, and community.

I have postulated that the curriculum practices identified are representative of the kinds of behaviors that curriculum specialists engage in or perform. Most important, they are measurable and observable behaviors for theorists and practitioners to study, and possibly use for assessment in school settings.

As the field of curriculum seeks to identify a compendium of operational roles, this quantifiable knowledge base of domains and practices might be helpful in defining what curriculum specialists should know and be able to do. Analyzing the frequency and conditions under which these behaviors can be observed in real situations and the degree to which they are emphasized in schools and classrooms might extend our understanding of the empirical relationships between theory and practice and promote successful implementation of school improvement processes

It is recognized that I have made two assumptions perhaps controversial in nature, that the **domains** represent the broad content areas that practitioners should know and be able to utilize in actual situations and **practices** refer to the specific roles of curriculum specialists and supervisors. In order to implement successful school improvement action plans, there will need to be agreement concerning domains and practices so that objective and quantifiable criteria can be clearly established. Currently many curriculum processes and decisions are made in nonconsensual ways. An agreed upon set of domains and practices should benefit the field of curriculum.

This study was an attempt to establish an empirical format for identifying **curriculum domains** (the knowledge base or important content areas of the field) and **curriculum practices** (precise activities curriculum specialists perform). Identifying the important content areas in curriculum, is essential to specifying the kinds of skills and behaviors that curriculum workers should acquire as a result of their post secondary education. Post secondary education departments and colleges of education should take a leadership role in establishing criteria that define professional standards. These programs should implement accountability measures that ensure that graduates have acquired the necessary skills for real world applications of curriculum. By creating standards for professional practice and producing competent curriculum workers, post secondary programs of education can play an integral role in helping schools to successfully implement school improvement initiatives.

The curriculum knowledge base of practitioners will probably differ from the professional knowledge base advocated by curriculum textbooks. Knowledge bases within curriculum textbooks are more likely to be akin to that of academicians in universities and colleges who conduct research and produce scholarship related to schools and practitioners. Establishing a quantifiable knowledge base, might serve as a catalyst for codifying the type of curriculum based technical skills and content knowledge that practitioners should acquire. This knowledge base might also suggest a compendium of generalizable knowledge and skills that has broad applicability and assists them in addressing new situations as well as traditional events. A susbstantitative knowledge base should include a repertoire that requires curriculum workers to know how to act instead of simply knowing about concepts.

The domains that have been defined and discussed within the context of a knowledge base are not simple discrete behaviors that have either a singular purpose or application. They should be viewed as components of a larger and more complex picture that requires curriculum workers to analyze the focus or outcomes they seek to attain whereby they may view these practices as tools for analysis and problem solving. Each of the domains and practices contributes to the sum of activities and roles that curriculum workers assume.

The intent of the domains and practices is to provide curriculum workers with the tools that constitute a broad base of understanding and skills that allows them to address emergent and practical curriculum related problems and tasks. For example, a curriculum worker involved in developing a curriculum guide for elementary mathematics might consider practices in the domains of curriculum evaluation, curriculum philosophy and curriculum policy. An individual who is identifying course objectives might incorporate practices in the domains of curriculum philosophy, curriculum evaluation, and curriculum design. Using this compendium as an instrument for teacher evaluation, a principal might consider practices in the domains of curriculum evaluation, curriculum design, curriculum development, curriculum philosophy to identify the strengths and weaknesses of a teachers' instructional behaviors. If this compendium is utilized as a tool for evaluating the overall curriculum within a school, several of the domains and related practices might be used to provide insight about the effectiveness of the overall curriculum.

This compendium of nine domains and 55 related practices might also serve as a template for graduate program development or certification programs in curriculum. Finally the domains might be used to develop course materials, program planning and identifying outcomes.

Summary

Using open and closed ended survey approaches, this research study identified a quantifiable knowledge base of important domains and related curriculum practices in textbooks and a list of the most influential textbooks in curriculum. The results demonstrated moderate to high levels of homogeneity among the Midwest teachers in their ratings of the importance of the domains of curriculum and related practices. The results demonstrated low to high levels of homogeneity among the Southeast teachers in their ratings of the importance of the domains of curriculum and related practices. The findings in this study also showed that the Professors of Curriculum tended to select textbooks that advocated the curriculum practices that they identified as most important.

This chapter presented a description of the professors' selections in the textbook and domain's survey, provided an interpretation of the results in relationship to the research questions and discussed the potential limits of the study. The implications of these findings were also discussed in terms of curriculum practice and research studies.

---

[5] I wish to acknowledge Dr. O. L. Davis for his comments regarding influential textbooks and the impact of curriculum textbooks.

BIBLIOGRAPHY

American Heritage Dictionary (1983). New York, New York: Dell Publishing Company.

Apple, M. W. (1988). *Teachers and Texts: A Political Economy of Class and Gender Relations in Education.* New York, New York: Routledge.

Armbuster, B. B. and Anderson, T. H. (1988). On Selecting "Considerate" Content Area Textbooks. *Remedial and Special Education* 9 (1), 47-52.

Ary, D., Jacobs, L.C., and Razavieh, A. (1990). *Introduction to Research in Education.* New York, New York: Holt, Rinehart and Winston.

Beauchamp, G. (1981). *Curriculum Theory.* Fourth Edition. Itasca, Illinois: Peacock.

Beauchamp, G. (1971-1973). Basic Components of a Curriculum Theory. *Curriculum Theory Network,* 10, 16-22.

Behar, L. (1992). *A Study of Domains and Subsystems in the Most Influential Textbooks in the Field of Curriculum 1970-1990.* Unpublished doctoral dissertation. Chicago, Illinois: Loyola University of Chicago.

Behar, L. and Ornstein, A.C. (1992). An overview of curriculum: The theory and practice. *National Association of Secondary School Principals Bulletin.*, Reston, Virginia. 76 (547) 32-44.

Bernstein, H. T. (1985). The New Politics of Textbook Adoption. *Education Digest,* 51, 12-15.

Bertilson, H.S. (1983, October). *Inaccuracy of Knowledge Represented in College Textbooks: Aggression as an Example.* Paper presented at the Northern Rocky Mountain Educational Research Association Meeting, Jackson Hole, Wyoming. (Eric Document Reproduction Service No . ED 2 69 995) .

Cheney, L. V. (1988). *American Memory.* Washington, D.C.: National Endowment for the Humanities.

Cody, C. (1990). The Politics of Textbook Publishing, Adoption and Use in *Textbooks and Schooling in the United States.* Eighty-ninth Yearbook of the National Society for the Study of Education. Chicago, Illinois: The University of Chicago Press.

Cole, J.Y., and Sticht, T. Editors. (1981). *The Textbook in American Society.* Washington, District of Columbia Information Office. (ERIC Document Reproduction Service No. ED 225 185).

Cronbach, L.J. (1984). *Essentials of Psychological Testing.* New York, New York: Harper and Row, Inc.

Doll, R.C. (1989). *Curriculum Improvement: Decision Making and Process.* Seventh Edition. Boston, Massachusetts: Allyn and Bacon.

Duin, A.H. and Prenn, M. (1985). *Identifying the Factors that Make Expository Text More Comprehensible.* (ERIC Document Reproduction Service No. ED 272 856)

Eisner, E.W. (1985). *The Educational Imagination: On the Design and Evaluation of School Programs.* Second Edition. New York, New York: Macmillan.

Eisner, E.W. (1987). Why Textbooks Influence Curriculum. *Curriculum Review, 26,* 11-13.

English, F.W., Ed. (1983). *Fundamental Curriculum Decisions.* Alexandria, Virginia: Association for Supervision and Curriculum Development.

English, R. (1980). The Politics of Textbook Adoption. *Phi Delta Kappan, 62* (4). 275-280.

Fraley, A. (1981). *Schooling & Instruction: The Rhetoric and the Reality.* New York, New York: Tyler Gibson Publishers.

Galluzzo, G.R. and Pankratz. R.S. (1990). Five Attributes of a Teacher Education Program Knowledge Base. *Journal of Teacher Education.* 41 (4). 7-14.

Gideonse, H.D. (1989). *Relating Knowledge to Teacher Education: Responding to NCATE'S Knowledge Base and Related Standards.* New York, New York: American Association of Colleges for Teacher Education

Giroux, H.A., Penna, A.N. & Pinar, W.F. (1981) . *Curriculum & Instruction: Alternatives in Education.* Berkeley, California: McCutchan.

Gronlund, N.E. & (1990). *Measurement and Evaluation in Teaching.* Sixth Edition. New York, New York: Macmillan.

Gudmundsdottir, S. (1991). Values in Pedagogical Content Knowledge. *Journal of Teacher Education.* 41 (3) 44-52 .

Hubbuch, S. M. (1989). The Trouble with Textbooks. *The High School Journal.* 72 (4), 203-209.

Husen, T. and Postlethwaite, T.N. (1985). *The International Encyclopedia of Education.* Oxford, England: Pergamon Press.

Johnson, M. J. (1976). An Invited Response to "What Curriculum for Graduate Instruction in Curriculum? Part 1". *Curriculum Inquiry,* 6 (1), 83-87.

Johnson, M. J. (1970-1971). Appropriate Research Directions in Curriculum & Instruction. *Curriculum Theory Network,* 6. 24-37 .

Johnson, M. J. (1968-1970). On the Meaning of Curriculum Design. *Curriculum Theory Network,* 3. 3-9.

Keith, S. (1985). Choosing Textbooks: A Study of Materials Selection processes for Public Education. *Book Research Quarterly,* 1 (Summer) 24-37.

Kerlinger, F.N. (1986). *Foundations of Behavioral Research*. Third Edition. Orlando, Florida: Holt, Rinehart, and Winston.

Kimpston, R. D. (1986). A Framework for Curriculum Research. *Curriculum Inquiry*, 16 (4), 463-474.

Komoski, P.K. (1980). *What Curriculum Leaders Need to Know About Selecting Instructional Materials*. Paper presented at the Annual Meeting for Supervision and Curriculum Development. (35th, Atlanta, Georgia. March 29-April 2, 1980.) (ERIC Document Reproduction Service No. ED 184 146).

Madaus, F. and Stufflebeam, D. Editors. (1988). *Educational Evaluation: Classic Works of Ralph W. Tyler*. Norwell, Massachusetts: Kluwer Academics.

Marshall, J.D. (1986). *The Politics of Curriculum Decisions Manifested through the Selection and Adoption of Textbooks for Texas*. Doctoral dissertation. University of Texas. (ERIC Document Reproduction Service No. ED 270 900).

McCutcheon, G. (1988). "Curriculum Theory and Practice: Considerations for the 1990s and Beyond." *National Association for Secondary School Principals Bulletin.*, Reston, Virginia. 72 (509) 33-42.

McNeil, J. D. (1990). *Curriculum: A Comprehensive Introduction*. Fourth Edition. Glenview, Illinois: Scott, Foresman.

Norusis, M.J. (1988). *The SPSS Guide to Data Analysis for SPSS-X*. Chicago, Illinois: SPSS, Inc.

Ornstein, A.C. (1990). *Strategies for Effective Teaching*. New York, New York: Harper & Row.

Ornstein, A.C. and Hunkins, F. (1993). *Curriculum: Foundations Principles & Issues*. Second Edition. Englewood Cliffs, New Jersey: Prentice-Hall.

Ornstein, A.C. (1987). The Field of Curriculum. What Approach? What Definition? *High School Journal.* 70 (4), 208-216.

Ornstein, A.C. (1986). Curriculum, Instruction, and Supervision--Their Relationship and the Role of the Principal. *National Association of Secondary School Principals Bulletin.* Reston, Virginia. 70(489). 74-81.

Payne, D.A. (1974). *The Assessment of Learning: Cognitive and Affective.* Lexington, Massachusetts: District of Columbia Heath and Company.

Perrucci, R. (1982). *The Failure of Excellence in Textbooks.* Paper presented at the Annual Conference of the American Sociological Association. (San Francisco, California. September 6-10, 1982). (ERIC Document Reproduction Service No. ED 233963).

Popham, W. J. (1990). *Modern Educational Measurement: A Practitioner's Perspective.* Boston, Massachusetts: Allyn and Bacon.

Ravitch, D. and Finn, Jr. C. E. (1987). *What Do Our 17 Year Olds Know?* New York: Harper and Row.

Rogan, J. and Luckowski J. (1990). Curriculum Texts: The Portrayal of the Field. *Journal of Curriculum Studies,* 22 (1), 17-39.

Rosales-Dordelly, C.L. and Short, E. (1985). *Curriculum Professors Specialized Knowledge.* Lanham, Maryland: University of America Press.

Saylor, J.G., Alexander, W.M. & Lewis, A.J. (1981). *Curriculum Planning for Better Teaching and Learning.* Fourth Edition, New York, New York: Holt, Rinehart, & Winston.

Schubert, W . H . (1984) . *Curriculum Books: The First Eighty Years.* Lanham, Maryland: University Press of America, Inc.

Schubert, W.H. (1986). *Curriculum: Perspectives and Practice.* New York, New York: Macmillan.

Sewall, G. T. (1988). American History Textbooks: Where do we go from Here? *Phi Delta Kappan.* 69 (8), 552-558.

Shane, H. (1981). Significant Writings That Have Influenced the Curriculum: 1906-81. *Phi Delta Kappan.* 62 (5), 311-314.

Short, E.C. (1983). The Forms & Use of Alternative Curriculum Development: Strategies: Policy Implications. *Curriculum Inquiry.* 6 (3), 43-64.

Short, E.C. (1984). *Organizing What We Know About Curriculum.* Manuscript paper written at The Pennsylvania State University.

Siegel, S. and Castellan, Jr., N.J. (1988) . *Nonparametric Statistics for the Behavioral Sciences.* Second Edition. New York, New York: McGraw-Hill.

Sosniak, L. A. and Stodolsky, S. S. (1993). Teachers and Textbooks: Materials Use in Four Fourth Grade Clasrooms. *The Elementary School Journal.* 93 (3), 249-275.

SPSS-X Inc. (1988). *SPSS-X User's Guide.* Third Edition, Chicago, Illinois: SPSS, Inc.

Stufflebeam, D., Foley, W. Gephart, W. Guba, E., Hammond, R., Merriman, H. and Provus, M. (1971*). Educational Evaluation and Decision Making.* Itasca, Illinois: F.E. Peacock.

Taba, H. (1962). *Curriculum Development: Theory and Practice.* New York, New York: Harcourt, Brace and World.

Tanner, D. and Tanner, L. N. (1980*). Curriculum Development: Theory into Practice.* Second Edition. New York, New York: Macmillan.

Tanner, D. and Tanner, L. (1990). *History of the School Curriculum.* New York, New York: Macmillan.

Tanner, L., Ed. (1988). *Critical Issues in Curriculum*. Eighty-Seventh Yearbook of the National Society for the Study of Education. Chicago, Illinois: The University of Chicago Press.

Thompson, P.J. (1987). *Writing a Textbook: From Theoretical Knowledge to Tacit Knowledge -- And Back Again!* Paper presented at the Annual Meeting of the American Educational Research Association. (Washington, District of Columbia, April 20-24, 1987). (ERIC Document Reproduction Service No ED 289 170).

Thorndike, R.M., Cunningham, G.K. Hagen, E.P. and Thorndike, R.L. (1991). *Measurement and Evaluation in Psychology and Education*. Fifth Edition. New York, New York: Macmillan.

Tuckman, B. W. (1988). *Conducting Educational Research*. Third Edition. Orlando, Florida: Harcourt, Brace and Javanovich, Inc.

Tulley, M.A. and Farr, R. (1985). Textbook Adoption: Insight, Impact, and Potential. *Book Research Quarterly* 1 (Summer), 4-11.

Tyler, R.W. (1949). *Basic Principles of Curriculum and Instruction*. Chicago, Illinois: University of Chicago Press.

Tyler, R.W., Gagne, R.M. and Scriven, M. (1967). *Perspectives of Curriculum Evaluation. Chicago,* Illinois: Rand McNally.

Tyson, H. & Woodward, A. (1989). Why students aren't learning very much from textbooks. *Educational Leadership.* 47 (3) 14-17.

Tyson-Bernstein, H. (1988). *A conspiracy of good intentions: America's textbook fiasco*. Washington, D.C.: Council for Basic Education.

Warming, E.O. (1982). *Encyclopedia of Educational Research*. Fifth Edition. New York, New York: Macmillan.

Woodward, A. and Elliot, D.L. (1990). *Textbooks: Consensus and Controversy in Textbooks and Schooling in the United States.* in D. L. Elliot & A. Woodward (Eds). Textbooks and Schooling in the United States. (Eighty-ninth Yearbook of the National Society for the Study of Education, Part 1 (pp. 146-161). Chicago, Illinois: National Society for the Study of Education.

Zais, R.S. (1976). *Curriculum: Principles and Foundations.* New York, New York: Thomas Y. Crowell Company, Inc.

Appendix A

Textbook Survey

DIRECTIONS: The survey below is divided into two parts. Part I deals with background data. Part II deals with a listing of curriculum textbooks*.

PART I: Please indicate the appropriate answer for each question.

1. Sex: M _____   F _____

2. Is your doctorate in curriculum and/or instruction?
YES _____   NO _____

3. What year did you earn your doctorate?
Before 1941____; 1941-1950_____ ; 1951-1960 _____ ; 1961-1970 _____ ; 1971-1980 _____ ; 1981-1990_____

4. Name the institution where you received your doctorate.

_____

5. Name the institution with which you are currently affiliated.

_____

PART II: List the textbooks published between 1970 and 1990 which you believe have had the most impact upon the field of curriculum. (List as many as ten. Ranking is unimportant)

1._____
2._____
3._____
4._____
5._____
6._____
7._____
8._____
9._____
10._____

* = A textbook is a book used for the study of a particular subject and is designed to explain basic information of a field including theory, research and practice.

Appendix B

Domains of Curriculum: Teachers' Survey

DIRECTIONS: Rate the items listed below using the following scale: [5] very important; [4] fairly important; [3] some importance; [2] fairly unimportant; [1] very unimportant. Circle the number that most nearly represents your opinion.

1. Reflecting upon schools of thought including: perennialism; essentialism; progressivism; reconstructionism; and existenialism.   1 2 3 4 5
2. Determines what changes took place as are result of the curriculum.   1 2 3 4 5
3. Attempts to define what subject matter will be used.   1 2 3 4 5
4. Determines the ends of education.   1 2 3 4 5
5. Provides information about the effectiveness of the curriculum.   1 2 3 4 5
6. Creates statements that give meaning to a school curriculum.   1 2 3 4 5
7. Uses techniques of science or logic to present a systematic view of phenomena.   1 2 3 4 5
8. Guides program development for individual students.   1 2 3 4 5
9. Determines whether actions yielded predicted results.   1 2 3 4 5
10. Selects subject matter and learning experiences.   1 2 3 4 5
11. Determines if objectives have been met.   1 2 3 4 5
12. Establishes the primary focus of subject matter.   1 2 3 4 5
13. Determines an orientation to curriculum.   1 2 3 4 5
14. Deals with structuring knowledge.   1 2 3 4 5
15. Influences the control of the curriculum.   1 2 3 4 5
16. Permits curriculum ideas to function.   1 2 3 4 5
17. Integrates careful planning.   1 2 3 4 5
18. Describes past curriculum thought and practices.   1 2 3 4 5
19. Recommends what learning experiences to include.   1 2 3 4 5

Appendix B contd

20. Offers suggestions for curriculum modification.	1 2 3 4 5
21. Develops curriculum guides.	1 2 3 4 5
22. Measures discrepancies between predetermined objectives and outcomes.	1 2 3 4 5
23. Analyses resisting and supporting forces.	1 2 3 4 5
24. Suggests a view of society and students in relationship to education.	1 2 3 4 5
25. Indicates instructional strategies to be utilized.	1 2 3 4 5
26. Identifies how students learn.	1 2 3 4 5
27. Advances hypotheses and assumptions of the field.	1 2 3 4 5
28. Interprets past curriculum practice.	1 2 3 4 5
29. Develops school grants.	1 2 3 4 5
30. Promotes curriculum planning and implementation.	1 2 3 4 5
31. Uses systematic inquiry for the purpose of solving a particular problem.	1 2 3 4 5
32. Provides a chronology of important events in curriculum.	1 2 3 4 5
33. Determines procedures necessary for curriculum plan.	1 2 3 4 5
34. Addresses question of who will be involved in curriculum construction.	1 2 3 4 5
35. Organizes patterns and structures of curriculum.	1 2 3 4 5
36. Attempts to integrate theory and practice.	1 2 3 4 5
37. States the purposes of education.	1 2 3 4 5
38. Elaborates on the theory of curriculum.	1 2 3 4 5
39. Judges worth of instructional methods and materials.	1 2 3 4 5
40. Mandates school goals.	1 2 3 4 5
41. States what ought to be taught.	1 2 3 4 5
42. Uses principles and rules to study curriculum.	1 2 3 4 5
43. Determines desired outcomes of instruction.	1 2 3 4 5
44. Communicates with local and state government agencies.	1 2 3 4 5
45. Improves curriculum programs.	1 2 3 4 5

Appendix B contd

46. Analyzes steps to be taken in problem
solving.   1 2 3 4 5
47. Determines effectiveness of curriculum
content.   1 2 3 4 5
48. Integrates content and learning experiences.   1 2 3 4 5
49. Decides nature and organization of
curriculum.   1 2 3 4 5
50. Focuses on research and/or inquiry of
curriculum.   1 2 3 4 5
51. Analyzes structures of curriculum.   1 2 3 4 5
52. Ascertains whether outcomes are the result
of the curriculum.   1 2 3 4 5
53. Determines criteria to measure success of
curriculum plan.   1 2 3 4 5
54. Examines forces that inhibit curriculum
innovations.   1 2 3 4 5
55. Identifies strengths of curriculum content.   1 2 3 4 5

Appendix C

Domains of Curriculum:
Professors' of Curriculum Survey

Part I

DIRECTIONS: Using the twelve textbooks listed below, select the one with which you are most familiar. Indicate your selection by circling the corresponding letter.

A. Apple	*Ideology & Curriculum*
B. Eisner	*The Educational Imagination*
C. Eisner & Vallance	*Conflicting Conceptions of Curriculum*
D. Giroux, Penna & Pinar	*Curriculum and Instruction*
E. Goodlad	*A Place Called School*
F. Goodlad	*Curriculum Inquiry*
G. Kliebard	*The Struggle for the American Curriculum 1893-1953*
H. Pinar	*Curriculum Theorizing: The Reconceptualists*
I. Pinar	*Contemporary Curriculum Discourses*
J. Schubert	*Curriculum: Perspectives, Paradigms & Possibility*
K. Tanner & Tanner	*Curriculum Development: Theory into Practice*
L. Zais	*Curriculum: Principles & Foundations*

Part II

DIRECTIONS: . Read each statement below. Use the numbers listed on the left-hand side and rank the importance of each curriculum practice (or item) based on your opinion. Use the following scale: [5] = very important; [4] = fairly important; [3] = some importance; [2] = fairly unimportant- [1] = very unimportant. Using the numbers listed on the right-hand side, rate the extent to which each of these curriculum practices (or items) are covered in the textbook with which you are most familiar, and use the following scale: [5] = very great extent; [4] = great extent; [3] = some extent; [2] = little extent- and [1] = very little extent. Circle the number that most nearly represents your opinion.

Appendix C contd

<u>IMPORTANCE</u>   <u>EXTENT</u> <u>COVERED</u>

IMPORTANCE		EXTENT COVERED
1 2 3 4 5	Reflecting upon schools of thought including: perennialism; essentialism; progressivism; reconstructionism; and existenialism.	1 2 3 4 5
1 2 3 4 5	Determines what changes took place as a result of the curriculum.	1 2 3 4 5
1 2 3 4 5	Attempts to define what subject matter will be used.	1 2 3 4 5
1 2 3 4 5	Determines the ends of education.	1 2 3 4 5
1 2 3 4 5	Provides information about the effectiveness of the curriculum.	1 2 3 4 5
1 2 3 4 5	Creates statements that give meaning to a school curriculum.	1 2 3 4 5
1 2 3 4 5	Uses techniques of science or logic to present a systematic view of phenomena.	1 2 3 4 5
1 2 3 4 5	Guides program development for individual students.	1 2 3 4 5
1 2 3 4 5	Determines whether actions yielded predicted results.	1 2 3 4 5
1 2 3 4 5	Selects subject matter and learning experiences.	1 2 3 4 5
1 2 3 4 5	Determines if objectives have been met.	1 2 3 4 5
1 2 3 4 5	Establishes the primary focus of subject matter.	1 2 3 4 5
1 2 3 4 5	Determines an orientation to curriculum.	1 2 3 4 5
1 2 3 4 5	Deals with structuring knowledge.	1 2 3 4 5
1 2 3 4 5	Influences the control of the curriculum.	1 2 3 4 5
1 2 3 4 5	Permits curriculum ideas to function.	1 2 3 4 5
1 2 3 4 5	Integrates careful planning.	1 2 3 4 5
1 2 3 4 5	Describes past curriculum thought and practices.	1 2 3 4 5
1 2 3 4 5	Recommends what learning experiences to include.	1 2 3 4 5

Appendix C contd

<u>IMPORTANCE</u>   <u>EXTENT</u> <u>COVERED</u>

IMPORTANCE		EXTENT COVERED
1 2 3 4 5	Offers suggestions for curriculum modification.	1 2 3 4 5
1 2 3 4 5	Develops curriculum guides.	1 2 3 4 5
1 2 3 4 5	Measures discrepancies between predetermined objectives and outcomes.	1 2 3 4 5
1 2 3 4 5	Analyses resisting and supporting forces.	1 2 3 4 5
1 2 3 4 5	Suggests a view of society and students in relationship to education.	1 2 3 4 5
1 2 3 4 5	Indicates instructional strategies to be utilized.	1 2 3 4 5
1 2 3 4 5	Identifies how students learn.	1 2 3 4 5
1 2 3 4 5	Advances hypotheses and assumptions of the field.	1 2 3 4 5
1 2 3 4 5	Interprets past curriculum practice.	1 2 3 4 5
1 2 3 4 5	Develops school grants.	1 2 3 4 5
1 2 3 4 5	Promotes curriculum planning and implementation.	1 2 3 4 5
1 2 3 4 5	Uses systematic inquiry for the purpose of solving a particular problem.	1 2 3 4 5
1 2 3 4 5	Provides a chronology of important events in curriculum.	1 2 3 4 5
1 2 3 4 5	Determines procedures necessary for curriculum plan.	1 2 3 4 5
1 2 3 4 5	Addresses question of who will be involved in curriculum construction.	1 2 3 4 5
1 2 3 4 5	Organizes patterns and structures of curriculum.	1 2 3 4 5
1 2 3 4 5	Attempts to integrate theory and practice.	1 2 3 4 5
1 2 3 4 5	States the purposes of education.	1 2 3 4 5
1 2 3 4 5	Elaborates on the theory of curriculum.	1 2 3 4 5
1 2 3 4 5	Judges worth of instructional methods and materials.	1 2 3 4 5
1 2 3 4 5	Mandates school goals.	1 2 3 4 5
1 2 3 4 5	States what ought to be taught.	1 2 3 4 5
1 2 3 4 5	Uses principles and rules to study curriculum.	1 2 3 4 5

Appendix C contd

IMPORTANCE		EXTENT COVERED
1 2 3 4 5	Determines desired outcomes of instruction.	1 2 3 4 5
1 2 3 4 5	Communicates with local and state government agencies.	1 2 3 4 5
1 2 3 4 5	Improves curriculum programs.	1 2 3 4 5
1 2 3 4 5	Analyzes steps to be taken in problem solving.	1 2 3 4 5
1 2 3 4 5	Determines effectiveness of curriculum content.	1 2 3 4 5
1 2 3 4 5	Integrates content and learning experiences.	1 2 3 4 5
1 2 3 4 5	Decides nature and organization of curriculum.	1 2 3 4 5
1 2 3 4 5	Focuses on research and/or inquiry of curriculum.	1 2 3 4 5
1 2 3 4 5	Analyzes structures of curriculum.	1 2 3 4 5
1 2 3 4 5	Ascertains whether outcomes are the result of the curriculum.	1 2 3 4 5
1 2 3 4 5	Determines criteria to measure success of curriculum plan.	1 2 3 4 5
1 2 3 4 5	Examines forces that inhibit curriculum innovations.	1 2 3 4 5
1 2 3 4 5	Identifies strengths of curriculum content.	1 2 3 4 5

NAME INDEX

SUBJECT INDEX

ABOUT THE AUTHOR

Linda S. Behar is an assistant professor in the Department of Educational Leadership at the University of Florida in Gainesville, Florida. She received her Ph.D. in Curriculum and Instruction from Loyola University of Chicago, an M.A. from Roosevelt University, and a B.A. from Lawrence University. Her areas of specialization include curriculum theory, policy issues in curriculum, special education administration and teacher education. She is published in *National Association for Secondary School Principals Bulletin, Educational Leadership, Florida Education Research Council Bulletin,* and the *Kansas ASCD Record.* She has been the author of an issue of the *NASSP Curriculum Report.* She is co-editor with Allan C. Ornstein of a forthcoming book tentatively entitled, *Contemporary Issues in Curriculum.*